M000034836

Beyond Breast Cancer

Alda Ellis

HARVEST HOUSE™ PUBLISHERS

EUGENE, OREGON

Cover by Left Coast Design, Portland, Oregon

Cover illustration by Vicki Kovaleski

Advisory

Readers are advised to consult with their physician or other medical practitioner before implementing the suggestions that follow.

This book is not intended to take the place of sound medical advice or to treat specific maladies. Neither the author nor the publisher assumes any liability for the possible adverse consequences as a result of the information contained herein.

BEYOND BREAST CANCER
Copyright © 2002 by Alda Ellis
Published by Harvest House Publishers
Eugene, Oregon 97402

Library of Congress Cataloging-in-Publication Data
Ellis, Alda, 1952–
    Beyond breast cancer / Alda Ellis.
       p. cm.
    ISBN 0-7369-0859-5 (pbk.)
    1. Breast cancer—Patients—Religious life. 2. Breast cancer—Religious aspects—Christianity. I. Title.

  BV4910.33 .E44 2002
  248.8'619699449'00922—dc21   2002001747

Printed in the United States of America.

02   03   04   05   06   07   08   09   10   / VP-CF /   10 9 8 7 6 5 4 3 2 1

To

Pat McClelland

She first gave me the opportunity
to be a part of something so meaningful.
She has instructed not only me but countless others
to walk with strength and courage.

Special thanks to all the ladies in this book
who have allowed me to paint their personal portrait stories.

And in
loving memory of my mother.

Contents

When the storms of life wreak unexpected havoc, when a shock comes out of the blue, hope cuts a tiny path of light through the darkness. Although breast cancer is a disease that strikes one in eight women, no one is ever prepared for the shocking diagnosis.

CHAPTER ONE

After the Rain Is a Rainbow

*Now faith is the substance of things hoped for, the
evidence of things not seen.*

HEBREWS 11:1

I'D BEEN FOCUSED ON MY FAMILY and on the business that my husband and I own and operate. I had a catalogue to put together
and showrooms to prepare, but now my computer was giving
me fits. For weeks I contemplated buying a new computer, a
painful option because I was so comfortable and settled with
my old one. Since I work out of my home studio, the computer
is a tool I use every single day. I knew how to operate, install,
delete, and create on my machine, but I was doing so with
increasing difficulty, my needs having simply outgrown its abil-
ities. My computer was like a favorite sweater or a pair of comfortable well-worn shoes—hard to let go of. But when my
screen froze one too many times, I finally made my move.

I gathered around me my computer-literate friends and
asked for their suggestions on what kind of system to buy. With
their advice, I ordered a new system. After the computer was
delivered to my house in all its pretty colored boxes, it looked
so easy to get it up and going—from the outside. But I still
dreaded opening those boxes and spilling Styrofoam everywhere. Later I found out that I was not alone in my hesitance.

When my sister had a new computer delivered to her house, it sat in the box for over a week before she even broke the seal.

After work one evening, my friend Michelle and I labored late into the night getting all the components—printer, scanner, monitor, keyboard, and processor—connected and plugged in. Because we also tried to read directions from time to time, we spent an entire evening pulling out my old system and plugging in the new one.

As the evening wore on, we finally heard a purr coming from the hard drive. My new computer was up and running at last. For the next two days, I sorted through files and struggled to feel comfortable learning new programs and reinstalling old ones. Far behind with my work and determined to start fresh in the morning, I labored diligently until 3:30 A.M. getting everything exactly where I wanted it.

Monday morning, I finally sat down with a sigh of relief, knowing everything was ready and would be all right. I could get back to work in earnest.

Looking out the window above my work desk, I enjoyed the view of a beautiful autumn day. Our hundred-year-old oak tree stood shimmering with its golden cloak of autumn leaves. Acorns were in abundance this year, and so were the squirrels.

A loud boom suddenly shattered the silence. I actually felt the walls and floor beneath me shake. Out of the corner of my eye I saw a flash of smoke, but I couldn't really tell where it was coming from. The electricity in our whole house had gone off, not to mention the electricity feeding my new computer, which had gone dark and silent.

I called the power company, which immediately dispatched workers to see what the problem was. No thunderstorm had rolled through our area; there'd been no bolt of lightning on this gorgeous, sunny, blue-sky day. There was simply not a cloud in the sky.

I stood outside on top of our hill, watching nervously down the road for the power company truck. Complete with extending bucket, the big white truck soon came rolling gently up our driveway, carrying a crew of men to assess the problem. Waving to the crew, I walked down our driveway to where the truck had stopped beneath a power pole. The workers only needed an instant to figure out what was going on, because right underneath our transformer, a dead squirrel lay stiffening on the ground.

"Here's your problem, ma'am," the repairman said. "Rarely do we see this happen, but the squirrel walking on the lines got electrocuted and blew the transformer. Give me about 15 minutes to repair it and install a new shield, and we'll have your power back on."

As I walked up the hill to our house and back into my studio, I worried all the way. My new computer. I just got it up and going—and it was almost done in by a squirrel!

I soon found out that because of precautions built into my new computer, the power outage had not erased my work. To my delight, nothing was lost. At the push of a computer button, I was right back where I'd been before the boom.

But I'd been reminded of my vulnerability.

The Yearly Mammogram

Like that squirrel's trek along the power line, my spiritual walk is sometimes fraught with unseen dangers. I am cautious, but despite all my precautions, my world can go suddenly dark. *Bam!* Not long after my mother died from breast cancer, I discovered through my yearly mammogram that I, too, had a lump that needed a biopsy. I felt like my inner transformer had just blown.

I tried to work in my studio. I tried to garden. I tried to keep busy—but nothing would keep my attention off my worry. At 2:30 in the afternoon, it was time to leave in my car and go get my eighth grader, Samuel, from school. I was thankful for that simple daily duty, because on some occasions after school, we stop for an ice cream cone. *This* was going to be one of those days. As we enjoyed our treat of ice cream, I listened as Samuel told me about his day. He'd had a substitute teacher in English and found his lost history book. Tomorrow there was going to be a field trip. Upon arriving home, Samuel put away his books and went outside to feed the horses, an after-school chore.

Because we live in the country and have lots of machinery on hand, I am used to hearing different sorts of motors. I heard the motor revving on the all-terrain four-wheeler as Samuel started it and raced down to the barn as usual. I walked into the house with Samuel's backpack and lunch kit and also with the additional burden of my worry about the news from my doctor. What would the biopsy show? After a few minutes, I heard the motor in high gear racing back up to our house. Samuel rushed in the back door calling me.

"Hey! Hey Mama! You gotta come see this!"

He wouldn't tell me his surprise, and I couldn't imagine what in the world Samuel had found as he asked me to hop on the back of the four-wheeler. Off through the wet woods we went.

Although the rain had stopped, the trees were still dripping water as we raced through the pasture gate, around the lake, over the mountain, through the woods, and into our open field of back pasture. Samuel came to a complete stop and turned off the motor.

"Look! Look up!" Samuel shouted. "It is the first one I have ever seen with both ends."

As I looked up, I understood Samuel's excitement, because the most gorgeous rainbow stretched out its arms over the sky. Samuel was thrilled to see a rainbow in its entirety. And just like Noah, I understood the rainbow as a sign of God's love for me.

The seat on the four-wheeler held us both close together, and I put my arms around Samuel in a big hug. We sat there looking up, naming the colors of every hue...purple, blue, yellow, orange, red. Thankful that my son wanted to share his discovery with me, I also felt grateful for the reminder that no matter what my future held, everything would be all right.

Even though your path may reveal many surprising turns and twists along the way as you travel through the woods and over the mountain, I hope to encourage your heart and light your way with hope. Because I actively engaged precaution by taking advantage of the latest technology in undergoing a yearly mammogram, I will be treated in the earliest stages of a disease that strikes one of every eight women. My mother was not so lucky. Her cancer was not detected until the very late stages, when the only thing doctors could do was help make her more comfortable.

I was still mourning my mother when doctors discovered my lump. In my case, early detection lightened what could have been a most difficult burden. And it drove home for me the most certain knowledge that breast cancer is not something we should be quiet about. This lurking threat—breast cancer—is something we as women need to be aware of and alert about. We need to talk about it, ask questions, and share what we learn. We need to support one another, pray for one another, and freely give our comfort and support. I am so thankful Samuel shared with me his wonderful discovery in the sky, because, truly, after the rain is a rainbow.

Hope in the Middle of a Crisis

All my life I have lived in Arkansas, which is the very heart of Tornado Alley. The terrible storms that bring tornadoes are a terrible part of our history. I can remember from my girlhood the quiet calm before the storm. When the storm began to gather, the dark gray, luminous clouds ushered in a sense of fear. Even now as a storm passes through, I stand on my front porch looking up to the sky, with the radio on in the background. I know the trauma such a storm is capable of producing.

Evening newscasts and Hollywood movies show the quick destruction wrought by a tornado. The camera scans over pieces of a home dangling from twisted tree limbs. Many citizens of our state have experienced firsthand the disaster that rips a home to pieces, sometimes leaving nothing at all but the foundation.

Shortly after we moved into our home, a tornado devastated our area, hitting us like an atomic bomb explosion. Miraculously, our home was only slightly damaged. A tree crashed into our bedroom, splattering glass everywhere, but the structure of our hundred-year-old house withstood the force of the storm.

Sitting on my front steps, I held my head in my hands and listened to a chainsaw. When I looked up through the maze of fallen trees, I saw a friend who had not been around in some time. He was not the only one who came by to help. Other friends and family members also gathered to pitch in and clear away the mess.

I understood what those good friends and family members were doing. With kindness, they were not only contributing acts of friendship or hard work, they were contributing hope. During all the years we have lived in our home, I have never forgotten what hope can mean in the middle of a crisis.

For many of us, the terrible storm of breast cancer is a part of our history. The moment our ears hear the news of a lump and the words *breast cancer*, we are in shock. Hope cuts a tiny path of light when, otherwise, it is only darkness that we see. Sharing these stories of the women who have gone before us can light our way and give us hope. It is my prayer that you can look to the light and find the blessings of faith and hope.

No matter what we think may be ahead, how difficult our journey, or how deep our pain, we have been blessed not only with the courage to endure, but also the strength to overcome our difficulties. As Christians, we have been given the sword of the Word of God—the understanding that through God, all things are possible. When the mountain seems too high to climb, we can simply say to that mountain, "Move, mountain, and get out of my way!"

God works so differently in each of our lives, and each woman's story paints a different portrait. The examples in this book offer a glimpse of how each one of us is different, yet our greatest need is one and the same…hope.

The author of Hebrews wrote, "…we might have strong consolation…to lay hold of the hope set before us. This hope we have as an anchor of the soul, both sure and steadfast…" (Hebrews 6:18-19).

I hope that through the blessing and inspiration that come from the stories in this book, each survivor will be able to hold high the torch and gather up the confidence to share her own story of life after breast cancer. May you offer kindness in another's trouble and have courage in your own. It is my prayer that this little book will help light your way, as you travel on your journey surrounded by God's love and the warmth of friends and family. May you hold steadfast to the light of hope.

Give yourself the best chance of survival through early detection—get a yearly mammogram. Gather hope to yourself through the Word of God and the love and support of family and friends.

*S*ometimes we think we have everything
in order in our lives when suddenly an unforeseen
event shakes the foundation stones of our faith.
At such a time, it is important to remember
whose hands our troubles are in.

CHAPTER TWO

In the Hands of God

Then David put his hand in his bag and took out a stone; and he slung it...

1 SAMUEL: 17:49

AS A CHILD, I LOVED THE STORY OF DAVID and Goliath and especially admired David's courage, which seemed bigger than the whole army of the Philistines. The Israelites showed concern for David because he confronted a giant with only a small slingshot. But to David, that giant of a man made a big target, so big that David knew he could not miss hitting Goliath with his slingshot and tiny stone. Using a stone of faith, we likewise can defeat the giant enemy of breast cancer. A slingshot in my hands is simply a toy, but a slingshot in David's hands of faith was a mighty weapon. What a slingshot can accomplish depends on whose hands it is in.

Sometimes unforeseen events enter our lives and shake the foundation stones of our faith. Recalling the story of David and Goliath that we were told in childhood is a wonderful reminder of how important it is to remember *whose* hands our troubles are in. Such was the case with Scott Mason when she suddenly found out she'd been diagnosed with breast cancer. Just like David, she knew that she could slay the giant, because her worries, concerns, and fears were in God's hands. Just like David,

Scott realized that no matter what the circumstances, God is bigger than any fear.

Scott's Story

When I visited Scott recently, she talked with me about her journey, including some courageous steps she took to find her way back from fear and doubt to trust and belief.

"It all started with simply trying to breathe better," she told me. "Because of lifelong allergies and a deviated septum, it got to the point where I could hardly breathe through my nose. I finally gave in and went to an ear, nose, and throat doctor to see what we could do. He thought we could alleviate the problem and improve my breathing, but it would take surgery, and after the surgery I would be out of commission for a bit."

Scott made herself a checklist, planning to catch up on everything before the surgery. She would get a haircut, have her teeth cleaned, and undergo her mammogram…because now was a good time to do it all. But the mammogram changed everything.

"On my mammogram," Scott recalled, "the radiologist detected a lymph node he had not seen before and suggested an ultrasound. The ultrasound showed a small lump that seemed so obvious. After he discovered it, it was very easy to feel, being practically on the surface. The nurse, the doctor, and I all looked at the pictures. I could tell the serious nature of the find by what the doctor did *not* say. Also, my husband is a doctor, and I've seen too many textbook pictures. I knew I might be in trouble."

Realizing that the lump would have to come out, Scott called her husband. He talked to the doctor, and the three of them decided to do the biopsy the next day. The hardest part was waiting for the phone call that would give the results.

"My husband did not believe this could be possible," Scott said. "I did not believe breast cancer was possible either, because I fit none of the criteria. I don't smoke, I eat healthy, and it does not run in my family. If you look at the risk factors, mine would be zero. Still, the shroud of fear was all over me."

The phone call finally came with the news Scott and her husband did not want to hear. Not only was the tissue malignant, the cancer was aggressive. Scott and her husband sat in their bedroom stunned by the diagnosis.

Telling the Children

They wanted to let their children know what was going on but could not find a good time to tell them right away. Their daughter had a friend spending the night, and the friend had lost her mother to breast cancer one year ago to the day. The little girl was already having a bad day, and Scott did not want to make it any worse. She decided to wait until the friend went home.

With her husband at her side, Scott finally told the children. She started with the mammogram. "I told them I had gotten some news and it was not good news, but it was not the worst news. I chose my words carefully, because I did not want to mince words nor keep it a secret."

She explained that she would undergo surgery in a few days, the doctors would be looking for more lymph nodes, and it would be worse if they found another lump. Together as a family, they would handle whatever news they were handed. "They sat sort of stone-faced, and I asked them if they had any questions," Scott said. "I kept talking and being as open with them as I could, but they were obviously shocked."

None of the three children had any questions. They each wandered off to their own bedrooms to digest the information they'd been given.

"In a little while, my husband walked down the hall and checked in on each of them. After he patted and loved each one of them, I went down the hall and did the same. Our oldest daughter was sitting with a highlighter pen in one hand and a tissue in the other, trying to study. My little middle child was silent. I could not get a word out of him. Silently, tears ran down his face; he just wanted to be quiet. Our youngest son was the most visibly upset and inconsolable, yet he was the one that all of a sudden had lots of questions. But he was crying so hard, he could hardly ask anything. I just held them all, trying to be strong for my husband and my children."

Scott did not realize how upset she really was until after the surgery. "I got the call that my lymph nodes were clear, and then I shed my tears. Those tears, however, were tears of joy, and I was saying thank you to God for my good news. That is when it all really hit me. I had been stoic in trying to hold everybody else together, because it hurt me to see my husband so visibly upset. I had never seen him so shaken, and I was trying to stay strong for him."

Going Forward

Scott continued to stay strong for her whole family. All along, she maintained a good attitude about having breast cancer. "I wanted everybody to know that you have to move on. This is what I have, and there is no going back. We can only go forward. Since there was nothing I would have done any differently, there was no looking back."

Scott made up her mind to do whatever the doctors wanted her to do. Youth was on her side. She was the mother of three young children, and those three children were depending on her. That in itself was reason enough for her to do whatever it would take—and move on.

"It's funny in a way," Scott continued, "because once I heard this news, I wanted to know—what did I do wrong? But there are no answers. While some cancers' causes are known, breast cancer is totally different. There has not been a verifiable cause found for breast cancer yet."

Because her husband is a doctor, Scott had access to more than the usual lot of books, and she steeped herself in reading. "I got to the point where I realized two things: first, I had to hold on to my faith, and second, I had to place trust in my doctors."

On Scott's first visit to her doctor, he explained the benefits of chemotherapy. "I could not understand why he was emphasizing it so strongly—as if he had to talk me into taking the chemotherapy. I wanted to know just one thing…when do we start? I guess, as I look back, he was just doing his job; some people do not have any treatment after the lump is removed. I wanted to do everything and *anything* I could do to lessen my odds of a recurrence. He explained the various treatments available to me, as well as their effectiveness in preventing the cancer's return."

Scott sat listening to her doctor talk. As she closed her eyes, she blurted out, "Just tell me when I can get started. Can I start today, or must I wait? You don't have to talk me into this. I am ready to get started *now!*"

Helping Others

Scott might easily have turned all thoughts to herself and her family. But instead, she broadened her view. Thinking about other women with breast cancer who would be coming along behind her, Scott considered how she might help someone else. She was willing to try new medicines, to serve as a kind of human guinea pig. "I know a lot of people do not want to do chemotherapy because of how sick they might feel," Scott said. "I was concerned about that, too. I knew there was so much new medicine out there, and I expressed that to my doctor. I even thought that whatever they want to do, we will try, because maybe it will help someone else next time."

I could hear through Scott's voice how she battled doubt. Doubt about how her cancer would turn out—would it be snuffed out, or would it raise its ugly head once again? Her family shared the same concern. Her friends also felt fear and doubt when she told them her news. Scott recalled calling one friend who at first encouraged her in a soft-spoken voice. "We hung up the phone, and she called me right back, hysterical. And that happened over and over again."

Other friends were also fine when she first told them her situation. Scott recalled, "They went about their work, and then they would call me back so upset. I shared my faith with them. I'd tell them that we cannot make our lives exactly as we would like them to be...no matter how hard we try. We can think that we have everything in order, and it just does not always work out that way."

Scott explained to her friends, "God gives our lives to us, and just when we think we have it perfect, something can dramatically change. We can have everything all mapped out, make our plans, but things will always change. Change is the one thing we can all be sure of."

Use This to Your Glory

I asked Scott if she ever became angry with God. At first she said no, she was never angry with God. But upon reflection, Scott remembered differently. "Well, maybe I was. I believed so strongly in God, but I was angry for the fact that I did not want my children to grow up without a mother, and I had trouble praying. I was not praying like I used to.

"I prayed differently. I would sit there and cross my arms, and I'd say, 'Okay, God. What? What do you want me to do? What is this all about? What do you mean I have cancer?'"

Scott smiled telling me she knew her conversation sounded like a child arguing with a father. When she finally worked through the anger, she was able to ask God from a state of peace, "What do you want me to do with this?"

A friend of Scott's gave her a book about women and strength in the Scriptures. Scott was so weak from chemotherapy that her friend would read the stories aloud. The friend also prayed with her, and in the act of praying together, Scott's prayers began to change.

"My prayer became not to heal me, or not to get rid of the cancer, but to use this to God's glory. I had decided to accept that even if I were not going to be healed, this was what I had. I have seen a lot of other people handle their cancer with anger, and some are so very angry and bitter. At the chemotherapy treatments, I could see the anger in their faces and how they did not want to be there. Well, I certainly did not want to be there either, but I knew I was not the one in control. I knew God was in control of my life, and my prayer just became— '*God, show me how you can use me.*'"

Help from Others

Scott braved her first chemotherapy treatment by herself. For the second treatment, about three weeks later, a friend called to ask if she could accompany Scott. "I told her I would be fine. There was no need for her to go with me. On the appointment day, she came by and knocked on my door and said that she would give me one more chance to say no. I melted and told her I would love for her to take me. Not only did she drive me, but she also stayed through the whole ordeal. She never left. She took me to every treatment and stayed with me through them all. I realize what a precious gift of her time that was, because even though I was only in chemo for six visits, over and over it seemed like eternity."

Family and friends were present with Scott during her most trying times, keeping her spirits up through humor and words of encouragement. Her brother talked recipes with the nurses and had everybody laughing. Friends both near and far sent cards and letters. Scott heard from people she hardly knew or did not know at all who were friends of her mother. Their kind words touched her heart and proved to be a wonderful dose of medicine.

Her friend Dede set up a food program and lined up friends to bring food for Scott's family three days a week. Dede started on day one, giving Scott a list of who signed up to bring what and when. "They even got instructions to put the food in disposable dishes so nothing would have to be returned," Scott said. "My children would answer the door when the friends and food started pouring in, and if I could at all I would sit there and talk to them a little bit…even with pillow marks on my face."

Scott found the scheduled meals to be a true blessing, something her whole family could enjoy together. Family and friends offered many gifts of kindness, sometimes in unusual ways. One friend had a real gift for thinking ahead, trying to protect Scott's time and energy.

But Scott said the biggest surprise came, again, from her friend Dede. "She alerted everyone who signed up to bring food that they would not receive a thank-you note. Dede emphatically said, 'Do not write thank-you notes, because everyone is well aware that they will not receive a thank-you note.'"

Instead of sending notes, Scott thanked each one personally. "That was just the biggest luxury, because we Southern women must write thank-you notes. Yet that thoughtfulness took the obligation off of me. I did not have to go get the stamps, get the stationery, write the notes, and get them to the mailbox. Little things just meant so much."

Scott tried to keep things as normal as possible throughout the whole ordeal of chemotherapy. "I was fortunate to have two drivers in our family, so school activities went on as scheduled and my husband could go on to work. There were track meets and soccer games that went on—I just have trouble remembering them. I probably even went to some of them, but I don't remember because the days after chemo were a very stressful time."

Chemotherapy, Hair Loss, and Prayer

Like most of the other women I talked with, Scott had to confront the issue of hair loss. She used humor and tried to have fun with it, but even with a matter-of-fact attitude, the loss was hard. She lost her hair and also her eyelashes and eyebrows. "Mine fell out like clockwork," she said, "because they told me that on the fourteenth day I would find that my hair would pull right out. I was on a trip to New York, and sure enough, my hair was just falling out."

Scott sprayed her hair stiff with hairspray, hoping that would hold the hair on her head until she could get home. She wanted her children to go through the change with her slowly, so that it would not be too much of a shock. Scott made it home with her lacquered hair and even had some left after shampooing out the hairspray.

Among the letters she received, Scott heard from other cancer survivors telling her that the worst part of everything is losing your hair. Scott decided to get one step ahead of the shock by shaving her head. Her children and husband gathered around her and tried to make it a family affair. "Although it was hard to find joy, we tried to make it funny."

Scarves were Scott's choice of headwear, but she also bought a fabulous wig. "I did not even try to duplicate my hair, because with my hairline, it could not be done. My new hair was a beautiful, long, blonde wig that was just ridiculous, but it was so much fun. My radiologist asked me if I had long blonde hair before, and I said yes—when I was in *college!* What the heck, I decided. Let's be 19 again."

People often did not know how to interact with Scott when she was out in public. Most people did not say anything. Once at a ball game someone told her she loved her wig. The next day one of the other mothers called Scott and apologized for what the other lady had said. Scott did not understand what she was talking about. The mother explained, "You know…she called it a wig."

Scott told her, "Well, that is what it is…a wig. I love my new blonde hair and that did not bother me at all." Scott began to feel bolder, because a lot of things no longer bothered her at all.

Her biggest luxury was wearing nothing on her head when she was home. "I talked to each of the children and asked them to please tell me if it really bothered them to see me without my hair. They were okay with seeing me without any hair, although it did take some getting used to for us all."

Besides hair loss, Scott learned to deal with other side effects of chemotherapy, not all of which were bad. The treatment, in fact, had a positive effect on Scott's allergies. "My allergies have just gone," she said. "Vanished. I used to be allergic to peanuts and corn, but when I got rid of bad cells, I got rid of good cells too. I got lots of new cells, and so it changed my allergies. I learned to be thankful for all things positive."

Exhaustion that came as a result of chemotherapy could be overwhelming, but Scott remembers lying in bed thinking, *I don't feel bad. The flu is a lot worse than this. Even a bad cold is worse than this.* "Yet I would just lie there. It was total fatigue. The chemotherapy takes a toll on a body, and it affects everyone differently. It does not cause symptoms like a regular illness. I was just very tired."

Even though Scott's immune system was at its weakest, she went snow skiing in Canada with her family. "Avoid germs. Don't eat fresh fruits and vegetables. Everything has to be scrubbed," Scott was told. "I would not even use someone else's ink pen. I did everything that I could to avoid someone else's germs, but I was determined to never miss a beat. So with careful attention, off we went.

"I wore a mask on the plane and in the airport. It was one of those that the doctors and nurses wear in surgery. Actually wearing the mask does not feel bad; it just does not feel normal. And when you see someone else wearing a mask, you feel bad."

If Scott sees someone wearing a mask now, she makes a special effort to talk to that person. For all the hours and hours she wore a mask in the airport and on the plane, only one person said anything to her the whole trip. "The lady simply asked, 'Why do you need the mask? Are you in treatment?'"

Scott responded, "Yes, I am doing chemo, and this is the time in the cycle when my immune system is weak." The woman followed up by, "You are looking good. Well, are you going to be okay?"

Scott told her with a smile, "I think I am. I think I am."

The exchange was brief but highly meaningful for Scott. "That was so uplifting to me for her to acknowledge that there was something wrong," Scott said. "I received so many stares, but her asking showed me that she cared, and her few words of encouragement meant so much."

Likewise, prayer from others was also a great comfort and benefit. "My friends and family would tell me I was on their prayer list, and that was so comforting to know. The fact that I was being prayed for in my friend Dede's Sunday school class, my brother's whole church, my little sister's Sunday school class, and all the other prayers not only lifted my spirits, but gave me comfort. I knew we were doing all we could do with the power of prayer. It made such a difference. I felt that I was nestled in faith and I knew God's arms were around me. Together we could handle whatever would come my way."

Scott wanted to go straight to the Word of God for encouragement. She found a source of strength in the little book of Scripture for women her friend had given her. "It was Scripture of hope that gave me comfort, and it helped me to get through my toughest days. When I could not read them, another friend would read out loud to me. This is what gave me peace."

Pass It On

Scott now regards herself as one of the most fortunate women in the world because through breast cancer, she found her way. "At 47, I am extremely blessed to have found my purpose in life. Some people live to be a hundred and still do not know why they are here. I do.

"I discovered I want to be there for other people who are going through a similar situation. My life is not about me, but it is about what I can do for others. I learned that a handwritten card, a spoken word of encouragement, or a kind deed, no matter how small, can make a huge difference. This is the lesson that walking this path has shown me. This is my purpose. I have been blessed by so many people that now it is my turn to pass it on."

Scott said she will never be able to repay all the kindness that everyone did for her...the cards, the flowers, the food. When she does something for someone now, they want to repay it. "I know how that feels," she said, "so I just tell them to pass it on. Just keep the kindness going and pass it on to the next person because I had to be the receiver once, and I intend to pass it on."

Like many women who experience breast cancer, Scott responded with a spirit of love and generosity. Her realization of purpose is a reminder for us all.

Jesus taught: "Do to others what you would have them do to you" (Matthew 7:12 NIV). Along with the story of David and Goliath, that Golden Rule is a lesson we learn in childhood. All too often, it is a lesson we leave behind. The difficult journey of breast cancer reminds us to remember and renew those early lessons.

Through prayer, you can walk from fear and doubt to trust and belief. Study the Word of God for comfort and guidance, and ask others to read aloud to you when you are overcome by fatigue. Maintain a positive attitude about your battle with breast cancer, and remember that you, like David, are in the hands of God.

Pass it On

Have you had a kindness shown?
Pass it on;
'Twas not given to you alone,
Pass it on;
Let it travel down the years,
Let it wipe another's tears,
Till in Heaven the deed appears,
Pass it on.

HENRY BURTON

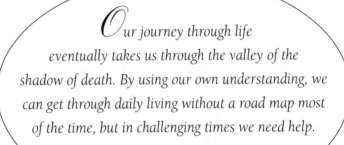

*O*ur journey through life
eventually takes us through the valley of the
shadow of death. By using our own understanding, we
can get through daily living without a road map most
of the time, but in challenging times we need help.

CHAPTER THREE

Spiritual Road Map

*Even though I walk through the valley of the shadow
of death, I will fear no evil, for you are with me;
your rod and your staff, they comfort me.*

PSALM 23:4 (NIV)

IN MY MANUFACTURING AND IMPORT BUSINESS, I travel a lot. Some trips involve driving long hours on the road. Some trips I fly and then rent a car when I arrive at the airport. Dallas, Atlanta, and Chicago are all cities that I visit frequently, and they are quite familiar to me as long as I stay on the main roads. I have a pretty good sense of direction, and there are always road signs to follow. I don't need a map, yet I carry one in the glove compartment of my car just in case.

Occasionally, I have to pull over to the side of the road, stop, and reach for that just-in-case map. The blue lines, red lines, and double lines with all the tiny numbers form a maze that I must ponder before I can figure out exactly where I am. I feel such a sense of relief when I find my destination on that map and see clearly how to get to where I am headed.

By using our own understanding, we can get through daily living without a road map most of the time, but in challenging times we need help. The Bible can provide that help.

One day I asked my friend Joyce McMullen if there is a particular scripture that speaks to her spirit. Her answer helped me realize that our faith walk can be like that road map, complete with landmarks, side roads, and main highways. Joyce answered quickly, "All my life I have treasured the twenty-third Psalm."

"Yea though I walk through the valley...?" I asked. As soon as I opened my mouth I felt silly for inquiring about the obvious, because I knew what she had been through. Joyce had walked through that defining moment of being diagnosed with breast cancer. She had walked through the valley of the shadow of death, just like so many other women.

Joyce's Story

Joyce's walk through the valley began five years ago when she was first diagnosed at the age of 52. Every morning, her day began with opening the doors of her bookstore, located in the small, charming town of Berryville nestled in the Ozark Mountains of Arkansas. Her plate glass window looked out onto the town square, where she saw a bit slower-paced life than the California lifestyle she had left several years ago. Hunter-green benches held old men in well-worn baseball caps swapping stories underneath the flagpole. With its post office, bank, and drugstore serving a population of only about 3,000 people, this little historic town has managed to maintain its turn-of-the-century charm. Joyce's bookstore, Happenings, was situated right in the stream of townspeople coming and going.

Since it was late November, people were scurrying about getting ready for the holidays. There was just so much to do…family members would be coming home to visit, and then there were the packages to mail to those who could not come. Besides all the decorating, baking, and shopping she had to do, to top it off Joyce had her annual Holiday Open House coming up at the bookstore. Right in the middle of her busiest season at home and at the store, Joyce got the phone call from her doctor's office telling her that she needed to come back in and talk with the doctor. This wife, mother, grandmother, and bookstore owner had been to the clinic earlier in the week for her mammogram, so she had a pretty good idea there was something on the X-ray image that was not supposed to be there. In confirmation of her worries, Joyce was told she needed to have a biopsy on the lump found through the mammogram.

Like most women, Joyce felt totally shocked by the news. "I just could not believe it, because breast cancer really did not run in my family. The only person I ever even knew of was my great aunt Annabelle. I could not feel a lump, and my doctor could not feel a lump. The only reason I had a mammogram was just to be on the safe side, and I am so glad I did."

Two years previous, Joyce had lost her mother during the Christmas holidays. Her mother's death had not been due to breast cancer, but Joyce decided not to tell anyone about her situation—not even her husband—because she did not want to have any more sadness during that time of the year. "In the back of my mind, I thought it would all turn out fine," she said. "But I was concerned. My faith kept me strong, and I kept my secret."

A very special customer visited the bookstore quite often, and the two women had become friends. This friend had undergone a mastectomy several years earlier, and had briefly mentioned it to Joyce. "She was the only person I knew who had breast cancer, and she kept my secret as I confided in her that I was going in for a biopsy. I guess I thought if I kept busy, it would go away, but of course it didn't. Through all our family gatherings, I was able to carry my burden in secret."

After the first of the year, Joyce told her husband and her sister that she needed to go in for a biopsy. "I am so glad I waited until after the holidays because the news turned out to be not at all what I wanted to hear. I was sort of numb hearing what the surgeon had to say, but I remembered the advice that the little elderly lady in my bookstore gave me, and how she strongly urged me to go to a breast center for treatment. If I did choose to go to a breast center, that meant a lot of driving time back and forth on the road, but I took her advice."

Joyce was given options with her treatment plan, and with the support of her husband and sister, she chose a mastectomy with reconstruction. "I am so pleased that I made that prayerful decision, because it was so nice to wake up from surgery and have a breast. Actually it is like having two different operations; I just had to go through with it once. The reconstruction that the doctors can do is phenomenal."

Her family gathered from around the country to offer their love and support while Joyce was in the hospital. Her surgery went well.

Small-Town Support

Joyce said she even returned to work at the bookstore a week later. She found the whole atmosphere of her small town to be supportive. Having lived in California and Washington, she had a point of reference with which to compare her life in Berryville. "Small towns are so great," she told me. "I was glad I moved back here where I used to visit my grandparents in the summers. I was on so many prayer lists—the Christian Church, the Baptist Church, the Methodist Church, the Church of Christ, and all our little small-town churches—that I had a real peace about the whole picture."

After word got out that Joyce had breast cancer, she learned that she was not the only one who had it, or even one of only a few. "I could not believe the women who would come to the bookstore and tell me they were survivors too. Some I had known for years, yet I never knew they had been through breast cancer. I did not have any idea how many women this disease had affected, but they would come to my store and share their own stories and offer words of encouragement. I got cards and letters from people I hardly knew, who were sincerely concerned and wanted to let me know they were thinking of me. I was so moved by the genuine caring attitude of the people in my small town."

Searching for Normal

Joyce started her chemotherapy treatments three weeks after her surgery. Everybody handles these treatments differently, and for Joyce, chemotherapy was the hardest thing she had ever done, with the weeks when she received her treatment the most difficult of all. For a while, she had to stop working. Her husband took charge of the household, one daughter took charge of the store, and another daughter also helped out. Joyce said the chemotherapy never made her nauseated—"I was just so tired."

She remembers the tiredness as the most difficult part. "When you are so busy all the time, running a business, running a family, running a home, and then you can't get out of bed…that is a hard reality to face. When I would try to get up, I would just have to lie back down. Finally after two weeks, I could get up for a bit."

Used to being energetic, Joyce now struggled with wanting to do too much. "The third week, I started going back to the bookstore for a few hours a day, and I learned that I must be a people person. It was so good for me to be back in the store and see everyone again. That is what is so wonderful about this small town. People really missed me and cared about me. That in itself was like a dose of medicine."

When I asked Joyce if she read a lot of books on breast cancer, she laughed. She is, after all, a bookstore owner. "Having a bookstore, you would think I would have read them all," she said. "Well, I did read quite a few, but I went through moods where I did not want to see anything on the subject. Then I would start reading again, anything I could get my hands on, and then I got tired of it. I think I was just searching for normal."

Yet there seemed to be nothing normal about what Joyce was going through. Like other women in chemotherapy, she had to deal with hair loss. Hers began falling out after the first chemotherapy treatment. "It started coming out slowly in my hairbrush, then by the handfuls," she said. "One morning I went into the bathroom, looked in the mirror, and ended up shaving my head. That was hard, but not as hard as watching it fall out by itself, because I got tired of it all over the shower floor and clogging up the drain."

Her daughters helped her pick out a wig, and Joyce handled it by coaching herself, "One day at a time. I will take this one day at a time. I am able to handle whatever comes my way because I have faith."

Joyce remembered the scripture that had kept her safe all these years—"Even though I walk through the valley of the shadow...." It helped her now to regroup and realize how much she had to be thankful for. "With that attitude," Joyce said, "I wore that wig through a very hot summer and fall. Finally one day, I took the wig off in the store, because wigs are hot, and I never put it back on again. My new baby-fine hair had begun to come back."

Taking Life up a Notch

In an outpouring of affection that came as a blessing, friends brought food, sent flowers, and mailed Joyce many cards. Knowing Joyce was too tired to read, her sister videotaped hours of the Discovery channel for Joyce to watch. Support from neighbors rolled in, and Joyce found herself the focus of all the prayer groups in town. Her husband took time off from his sawmill and stayed around the house. Her daughter kept the bookstore open every day. She even compiled a list of people who stopped by to ask how Joyce was getting along.

Family, neighbors, churches, and friends all supported Joyce on her road to recovery, and five years later, the people of her small town are still kind and concerned. Knowing that all these people really cared touched Joyce's heart. "My faith never wavered, and I decided I would take life up a notch and find the purpose to where this road was leading me," she said.

Her search for purpose started when she became good friends with a lady who worked at the bank. Joyce had known the woman as a customer, but one day she came to the bookstore and shared with Joyce that she, too, was a breast cancer survivor. Having been diagnosed just the year before, she offered to answer any questions Joyce might have. Joyce found her generosity and understanding to be a source of strength—and inspiration.

"I appreciated her sharing her story with me so much. In fact, we are now both volunteers for the Reach to Recovery program," Joyce reported. Both women took a training session by the American Cancer Society and now visit other patients who are recently diagnosed. They go to a class once a year to stay on the list, and visit when they are called to help.

"Even though we are in a small town," Joyce said, "it is amazing how often breast cancer is diagnosed. I think they are finding more because we are becoming more educated about having mammograms. There seem to be so many cases in our area...but people are surviving it. There is obviously not a cure, but we are surviving it. Now, helping other people go through what I did has become my purpose. I have been amazed at the flood of women who had breast cancer through the years and I never knew about it, because no one talked about it. Now we are talking about it and educating women.

"More women are coming forward who never would before," she said, and she has been deeply touched by the stories she has heard. "Even now, there is a sweet little lady in her seventies who has recently been diagnosed with breast cancer here in Berryville. Her daughter-in-law came and shared with me her story one day while I was at the bookstore. I went right over and talked to her and told her I would be there for her and help her get through this. Once breast cancer is diagnosed, there is so much more now that can be done than ever before. I knew she was not the type of person to talk about such a private matter, but I could tell that just my being there meant so much to both her and her daughter-in-law."

I asked Joyce if she felt like she herself had become a road map to somehow guide others through this difficult time. But she said, "No, my road map can be found in the twenty-third Psalm."

Joyce has been very blessed while traveling on her road to recovery. She never forgot where her strength came from, and now she is a blessing to many others across her rural area. She is on the board of directors of the regional affiliate of the Susan G. Komen Breast Cancer Foundation. She is an up-to-date volunteer in the Reach to Recovery program of the American Cancer Society and was awarded the Sam Walton Business Award along with Community Service awards as one of the ten most admired women in Carroll County, Arkansas for the year 2000. She is also active in the Relay for Life program. And although there is no official breast cancer support group in the small town of Berryville, stop by the Happenings bookstore on the town square. Joyce says that the door is always open.

If you've been diagnosed with breast cancer, investigate your options thoroughly. Talk to your doctor, members of your family, and other women who have been down that road already. Scripture is a spiritual road map that can help you get your bearings.

We don't have control over every situation
that happens in our lives, but we do get to decide what
to take away from them. Look for the lesson,
go on with your life, and let your light shine.

CHAPTER FOUR

Let Your Light Shine

Let your light so shine before men, that they may see your good works and glorify your Father in heaven.

MATTHEW 5:16

BETH MASON, OWNER AND FOUNDER of Smart Talk motivational seminars, spends her days consulting, coaching clients, delivering motivational keynote speeches, and conducting sales training seminars, and goal- and business-planning workshops. She is one of those who had not planned on taking time off to fight a war.

Her work life is filled with travel, taxis, hotels, and airports, and she has stood on stages all across the country sharing the secrets of sales success—through motivation, perseverance, and humor.

Beth, who entered the world of real estate in 1976, has risen to the top in three different cities, receiving numerous awards for her work. She won the Realtor Associate of the Year award in Fayetteville, North Carolina, and Sales and Marketing Excellence awards in Little Rock, Arkansas, and Washington, D.C. In 1991, Beth was her company's number one producer, beating over 6,000 agents in the worst real estate market the Washington, D.C./Virginia area had ever seen. That award brought national attention and recognition and translated into a whole new career for Beth. After being featured in a national real estate audio program produced by the Howard Brinton Star Power Club out of Boulder, Colorado, she soon became a popular keynote speaker and sales trainer for top corporations and businesses.

Companies listen as she encourages, motivates, and produces results for her clients. The miraculous part of Beth's story is what she doesn't tell you...the fact that while working in the real estate business she was attacked, viciously assaulted, and left for dead by a man later identified as a prolific serial murderer.

The courage to put all that behind her is in itself worthy of a medal. Beth feels strongly that what she learned from her experience ultimately enriched her life. The community and her friends so rallied around her that she was able to view the world as a wonderful place full of good, caring people who will be there when you need them.

Surprising everyone, she went back to work selling real estate shortly after leaving the hospital. Beth earnestly told me, "I had no control over what the man did to me, but I had total control over how it affected the rest of my life. I was not going to let him rob me of a minute of it."

Also, what you do not see in Beth's spirit is evidence that she was diagnosed with breast cancer. It seems that nothing can stand in her way.

When I spoke with Beth, she was dressed in workout clothes and was on her way to the gym. She looked trim and energetic, and her eyes were sparkling. One would never know by looking at her that she'd experienced the trauma of breast cancer.

The vivacious, energetic philosophy of her work is also true of her life's purpose—"Let your light shine." Beth told me she is happiest "when I know that I am letting my light shine, which for me is energetically taking knowledge that I have learned and handing it back to others."

Annual Mammogram

Beth didn't have a clue that her own light was about to flicker. The jolting news on her annual mammogram came as a complete surprise, as it does for almost everyone who goes in simply for an annual checkup. Like so many other women, Beth found herself on the receiving end of a personal crisis. But Beth was determined to turn her adversity into a beacon of light that shines forth for others, once again applying to her own life the principle that she lectures about in her seminars.

I learned from my interviews that each person handles her situation differently, and Beth's way of dealing with her illness is certainly her own, however much it may have in common with the journeys of other women. Beth shared with me some insights on going through diagnosis and treatment, and what brought her back to the top of the mountain after she had walked through the valley. Cloaked in the painterly light of God's love, she is truly a portrait of courage.

Beth talked about the many women who have traveled this road, where the bend in the road is not always a scenic byway…sometimes it is just a plain, potholed, dirt road detour. Although statistics show what a life-threatening turn the disease can take, Beth learned that one need not give in to fear. Through using wisdom and faith, fear can be omitted from the picture.

Upon hearing the diagnosis, Beth immediately asked all sorts of questions, not only of her doctors, but also and especially of her nurses. "The nurses," Beth said, "are just so helpful in answering questions about what to expect, what to do, and what not to do, because they seem to have more time to stop and listen to a patient's concerns. They can be so comforting as they share their knowledge, because they see [breast cancer] on a daily basis. My nurses were invaluable."

When her cancer was discovered, Beth had recently moved. A single woman with no husband or children, she found herself dependent upon the warmth of friends and family. Beth described to me how they blanketed her with kindness...from beginning to end.

She believes she did the right thing when she chose to share the news with her family and friends immediately. With her gift of humor intact, she wrote: "I had my annual mammogram on the seventh...right after I voted, and things have not been the same with me or our country ever since." (She was referring to the Bush-Gore political battle.) "Unlike the election, my results were immediate. In fact, I'll probably be through all possible and conceivable treatments before we even know who is the new president of our country."

Beth continued, "Bummer news is that they found a *thing*, but the good news is they found it. I have great doctors; they removed it the next morning, and it was as they suspected, malignant...but teeny tiny and contained. It was so weird. I had to say, 'I have breast cancer'...didn't feel like it, and I wanted to say I *had* it, as they took it out, but that is not how it works. Now we are in the testing phase. I have to have surgery again next Wednesday, and they'll take out some lymph nodes.

"Things are looking good so far...and I am not even worried about losing my breasts...they were not mine to begin with...and I figured I could just get more. And I figure no hair for a while in the winter won't be too bad...I could use a fake fur hat or two. After I read all the $150 worth of books I bought, and do even a third of the stuff they tell me to do, I will be healthier than I ever was. Sooo...my big new cause, as if I needed one, is annual mammograms!"

A Steady Stream of Friendship

> *A faithful friend is a strong defense; and he that*
> *hath found such a one hath found a treasure.*
>
> Joseph Addison

The cards, notes, letters, and E-mails came from friends across the nation as well as from students who had been in her classes. One friend and former student E-mailed her immediately on getting the news. She shared her own story with Beth.

On a morning shortly after she herself had been on chemo, the friend woke up to a substantial snowstorm. Schools were closed, kids were home for the day, and she was feeling pretty lousy. In the stillness of the morning, she thought a shower would make her feel better so she went into the bathroom. "I stood in front of the mirror and pulled my fingers through my hair. I came away with a handful of hair. I cried. I knew it was going to happen, but the reality of it still made me cry. And so I called my best friend, Beth. I was crying so hard, all I could manage to say was, 'It's coming out.'

"My life changed because of what Beth said. She didn't say, 'You'll look fine in a wig.' She didn't say, 'You knew it was going to come out.' She didn't say, 'It'll grow back.' She said, 'I'll be right there.'

"And somehow I knew that if I had a friend who was willing to drive six miles in a snowstorm at 6:30 in the morning to be with me just because my hair was falling out, God was giving me everything I needed to get through this ordeal...and he did."

That story exemplified the way Beth's own friends responded. They were there from the beginning, standing by whenever needed throughout the treatments, sending E-mails, notes of encouragement, and humorous love notes or stopping by to check on her. It was a steady stream...not necessarily a flood... of friendship.

"The biggest help that I could give somebody going through this," Beth said, "is to simply go by and say, 'What can I do for you today?' That is what my friends and family did for me. I was fine most of the time, but those days right after the chemotherapy, it was nice that my nephew just came over and spent the night so if I did not feel like getting up and letting the dog out, he could do it."

After her last chemo treatment, Beth was totally drained of energy. Dragging herself out of bed after several days spent doing only what was absolutely necessary, she walked into the kitchen to get something. "My sister-in-law had come over and cleaned and straightened my kitchen," she said. "It sparkled as the sunlight poured in. That is when I knew I was going to live."

Friends and family were at her side, bringing casseroles to her kitchen and flowers to her bedroom and leaving messages of encouragement on the answering machine. Their help was immeasurable. One of the messages Beth saved from a friend served to remind her that she was irreplaceable. "Grieve over your hair for a while, if you must," the note said. "Then forget it. It'll grow back, and you can rent some more in the meantime. We just can't rent another Beth."

Faith in God, the love and support of family and good friends, and the wisdom of her doctors and nurses—combined with a dose of time—all took Beth to the place where she could say: "What a wonderful year full of wonderful things to be grateful for: friends who care, sunshiny winter days, rain in the summer, my old dog, Bristol, who doesn't seem to mind being blind, and my puppy, Callie, who doesn't seem to mind being in trouble all the time, and their dog-breath kisses that wake me up every morning. My sisters, my brothers and their precious wives, and their individualities. Perennials in all colors. Spring. Love in general. I am thankful for friends who call and for having such special friends to call. Cell phones with cheap coast-to-coast rates, E-mail, jokes, and things that make me laugh. I am thankful for time with my mama, sitting on her deck overlooking the lake at daybreak.

"I am also thankful I have nieces and nephews to harass me, my home in Little Rock, airline frequent flyer miles, and the Starbucks in the St. Louis TWA terminal. I'm grateful for my honey's poetic ability and the flowers he sends. For medical science and specialists who are special. Friends bringing treats. A

Daddy who always knows where I am. I'm just so grateful, too, that I'm blessed with friends, girl friends, long-time friends, new friends, friends that pray, friends that give me energy, interesting friends, nice neighbors, different friends, friends that differ, and friends that make a difference. Friends with talents, friends that are generous, friends that share, friends in Virginia, Little Rock friends, friends across the nation, and life in general.

"Now here is my new leaf. I am hereby resolved to play more, take golf lessons, eat less, exercise daily, live fully, clean out my closets, take stuff to Goodwill, keep my E-mail address book current and up-to-date. I am going to read a book a week, balance my checkbook monthly, watch less CNN, conquer my free-minutes cell phone addiction, enjoy my nieces and nephews, improve my garden, keep fresh flowers on my desk, burn candles, listen to all my CDs, sit quietly occasionally, be my expressive self always, praise God openly, clean the garage, travel lightly, don my jewels, use my good china, evaluate before investing, and watch out for large trucks. [Beth's car had been totaled when hit by a big truck.] I will be an advocate for annual checkups. I'll sing out loud, always wear a smile, and do lots of other happy things."

Cleaning Closets

Beth struck a note of resonance in me when she talked about cleaning out closets. "It usually takes some event to urge me to dig in, such as the change of seasons, or time for a fresh coat of paint," she said. "It is not something that I look forward to doing, but it feels so wonderful after it is all over."

Like Beth, when I clean closets I find all sorts of things I have not worn in a long time, either because they were too small, too large, too short, or too long. I find things I thought I had lost and can now be enjoyed again. I am able to throw outdated papers away. And finally, in one recent cleaning, I was able to let go of the faded rose from an anniversary dinner and crayon drawings from my two sons. I chose to keep the plaster handprint, old Mother's Day cards, and the last letter from my mother. Such cleaning feels so good after it is all done; yet it feels even better to see the extra space in the closet.

There is something symbolic about cleaning a closet. Making room in a closet makes room for the future and helps us to realize there are some things cluttering up our lives— some of the things we hold on to that we really should let go of.

Beth reminds us that sometimes an event in our lives prompts us to clean out our closets a little deeper. "Breast cancer is just one of those jolts that helped me to clean out my closet. I realized what was really important to me, *who* was really important to me, and just what all it was that I needed to let go of. As part of simply growing older and wiser, there are just things that we don't need any more, and it takes a wakeup call to clean house. Letting go of anger, envy, and bitterness gave me a whole new way of making room for the things that had meaning, and all I wanted to hold on to."

The clutter in our closets can easily pile up little by little without our even realizing it, until something tells us it is time to look inside our hearts and tidy up a bit. And when we do, it feels so good.

What's Good About Having Cancer?

Beth also talked about coaching a couple who thought they were going to buy a business. "They had been considering this move for quite some time," she said, "but the purchase never came to fruition. So I asked them what was good about *not* buying the business. What is the lesson learned here? Now if you ask me what was good about having cancer, I could tell you several things."

Having breast cancer prompted Beth to make changes in her work life. She got off the road and doesn't travel as much. "It was almost like it gave me an excuse to do something I needed to do—for myself anyway."

Even though she doesn't have control over everything or every situation that happens, Beth realizes she does get to decide what to take away from each one. "I try to find a bit of purpose in each day. I try to find a little joy."

Beth looks at her days with an eye to the journey and tries to find the lesson. "In the goal planning classes that I host, we talk about the best way to predict the future—to *create* it. Yet we design our goals and plans not knowing how long our lives will be—even apparently picture-perfect, healthy ones. So, it is important that our plans allow us to accomplish three things, and this is my wish for you as we all step into this new millennium.

"May you fulfill all the goals in the new millennium that allow you to:

- enjoy your days
- secure your future
- and create the legacy you wish to leave.

It is my prayer that your days have joy and give your life purpose."

Beth is back on track, much wiser, more thankful, and inspired by the true caring of friends, family, and acquaintances. As Beth took her leave of me, heading off to the gym, she handed me a sack of water hyacinths from her water garden.

Beth offered great advice as she was parting—take care of yourself, but think of other people. Smart talk from a smart woman. Seems to me, Beth's light is back on again, shining brighter than ever.

⌒

Simple acts of friendship can provide you with a spark of life while you're dealing with breast cancer. Walking into a clean kitchen, opening a humorous love note, knowing that someone is there to take out the dog—all these can be ways of experiencing God's love. Accept these simple acts of devotion as gifts not only from your friends and family, but as gifts from the Almighty as well.

If I were asked to give what I consider the single
most useful bit of advice for all humanity it would be this:
Expect trouble as an inevitable part of life and when it comes,
hold your head high, look it squarely in the eye and say:
"I will be bigger than you. You cannot defeat me."

ANN LANDERS

*W*inning teams and winning
victories depend on teamwork. When goals are set
high and everyone works together, great races can be
won. When everyone shares a burden, the load is not
heavy for any one person. You are
not alone in your race.

Chapter Five

Race for the Cure

What we have done for ourselves alone dies with us; what we have done for others and the world remains and is immortal.

Albert Pike

My friend Vickey Metrailer and I attended college together and have remained friends through the years. Our sons went to the same high school, so our paths often crossed. This past year I enjoyed sitting back and watching Vickey in a new light—not that of mother, friend, or wife, but that of community leader.

One Sunday afternoon I flipped through the pages of our old college yearbook and looked upon her youthful, smiling face. Tucked between the pages was a dog-eared newspaper clipping about the legendary Alabama football coach, Paul "Bear" Bryant.

The coach was being interviewed on his achievement of all-time records in football. But in the article, never once did he take personal credit for winning, preferring instead to emphasize his team. "If anything goes bad," the coach said, "then *I* did it. If anything goes semi-good, then *we* did it. If anything goes real good, then *you* did it."

From reading the article, I knew that Coach "Bear" Bryant was a great leader, because he held high the claim that winning teams and winning victories depend on teamwork. When goals are set high and everyone works together, great races can be won.

Vickey Metrailer is a living testimony to that ideal. She may never have her picture in the newspaper surrounded by a football team, but she did have her picture on the front page of our state newspaper with a team of runners inspired to run a race—breast cancer's annual Race for the Cure.

Holding that dog-eared article in my hand and looking at Vickey's picture in the yearbook, I recognized the link between them. The winning words of a champion came not only from a giant of a football coach, but also from a petite wife, mother, and friend.

One Race We Can't Win Fast Enough

At the time of our interview, Vickey Hum Metrailer was chairman of Little Rock's annual breast cancer awareness race, the Susan G. Komen Race for the Cure, a 5K run (or walk). In 1980, Susan Goodman Komen fell victim to breast cancer at the age of 33. She died three years later. In addition to her husband and two young children, Susan left behind a sister, Nancy Goodman Brinker, who made a promise to Susan to dedicate the rest of her life to breast cancer research, education, and treatment. Nancy kept her promise, starting the Susan G. Komen Breast Cancer Foundation in 1982. Our community, like many others across the nation, embraced the foundation and all it stood for.

Through Vickey's prayerful leadership, Little Rock's community race caught national attention in 2001 because of the number of registered participants. A year's worth of planning came to fruition early one Saturday morning in September as 33,500 registered (along with many unregistered) women lined up along Main Street to begin the race. In her own quiet way, Vickey had inspired and motivated each one of those people through her leadership, spurred by the conviction that this is one race we can't win fast enough.

Vickey was pleased at the number of registered participants, but she was most pleased by where the ladies came from. "We had entrants from 300 small towns and communities. The rural women of our state were in attendance, and the minority population of African American women whom we were reaching out to came in numbers. We were reaching out to the small towns and communities and wanted to surround them with the support of our whole community."

The position of being chairman had consumed Vickey's time, talents, and energy every day for a year. In prior years she had played other positions on the team, leading up to the position that she now held as "head coach." She had been asked before to be chairman of the race but declined, saying that she would not chair until all her children were away at school. When that came about last year, Vickey took up the task. Her work on this project was enormous, yet just like that great Alabama football coach, Vickey never emphasized her personal contribution. Instead of the word "I" she always said "we."

"The funds we raise through registration fees are awarded to projects and programs," she explained to me. "These programs reach out to the community to provide assistance and incentives for screening and early detection. Our grants help to fund breast cancer research, provide counseling and support services, and, most importantly, help to fund educational programs on the importance of early detection."

So Many Ways to Help

Even though Vickey herself has not been diagnosed with breast cancer, some close to her have. Vickey described the teamwork involved in supporting one such friend, a woman with four daughters. "We got together several friends and put a plan of action in place to get the laundry done for her. You can imagine how much laundry four children can accumulate, yet this was such a little gesture on our part. When we all pitched in, it was not difficult on any one person, but it made a *huge* difference to a mother of four girls."

There are so many ways to help, Vickey said. No matter what friends' talents are, they can be of help. Whether it's providing food, doing laundry, writing cards, or driving someone to treatments, we all have the ability to help in some way. "When everyone shares a burden," Vickey said, "the load is not heavy on any one person."

I asked Vickey to describe race day. She told how she stood on a stage at the starting point watching the mass of people file past her for 20 minutes while the participants began the race. It was the most heartrending experience she had ever had. In that flood of faces, she saw a breast cancer survivor pushing another survivor in a wheelchair. The survivors are easy to spot because they all wear pink T-shirts.

"Some of the women had no hair," Vickey said, "only caps on their heads—and yet they came. All the other participants wear shirts with the race logo or their team logo. Some were holding signs labeled *In memory of* or *In honor of*. I saw survivors holding hands with their families. I would look down and see a face that I knew, and sometimes I was amazed that they would even register to be in the race. Then I would see a little girl and her mother walking together, which to me was a symbol for the future. I stood there so excited. It struck me as a constant flow of positive, peaceful energy. Standing there watching, tear ducts swelled and emotions came flooding. For me, that was a once-in-a-lifetime experience that can never be replicated."

A survivor parade followed immediately after the race. The Marine Corps color guard played, and the university choir sang as one survivor turned into two, and two into four, and so began a march of survivors clad in their pink shirts. The crowd moved in waves to the sidelines, clapping as the survivors walked in their own private walk.

"What just sort of happened," Vickey said, "will continue to grow."

The money from the race will help thousands of women, both through research and support programs. "We could spend every penny we earn on one person if we supported only treatment," Vickey said. "We support so many with our programs. It is like the old saying, 'You give a man a fish, you feed him for a day. You teach him how to fish, you feed him for a lifetime.' A lifetime of awareness, education, and prevention is what we are after—short, of course, of finding a cure for breast cancer."

Behind the Scenes

Next year there will be another race with a new chairman. When I asked Vickey what role she would play next year, she spoke with enthusiasm: "I will be involved in the formation of a corporate sponsor committee."

Her true love is working behind the scenes with the logistics of the race operations, getting everything to run smoothly. She cited two ladies, Wendy Saer and Pat McClelland, who have served as great examples. Following in their footsteps, she plans to help raise funds for the race through corporate donors.

Women such as Vickey, Pat, and Wendy, whether they have had breast cancer themselves or not, are all steadfast in their faith. Vickey exercises her faith in her daily walk with God. Her relationship with God is a part of everything she does, from raising her children to planting seeds through deeds that will produce fruits for future generations to enjoy.

Be steadfast in your walk of faith. Run the race to win, not only for yourself, but to glorify God. By helping others and accepting help from others, you can be part of a winning team. Good teamwork means everyone carries part of the burden. Put God at the head of your team.

Planting a Fig Tree

A queen riding along a road saw an old woman digging in her garden. Beside the old woman lay a young sapling ready to be planted. After the queen commanded her horseman to stop, she asked the old woman, "What kind of tree are you planting?"

"A fig tree," replied the old woman.

"A fig tree! How old are you?" the queen asked.

"I am 90," came the answer.

"You are 90 years old and you plant a tree which will take years and years to bear fruit?"

"Tell me," said the old woman, "did you eat figs when you were young?"

"Well, of course," answered the queen. "Why?"

"Who do you think planted the tree from which those gifts of fruit were obtained?" the old woman asked.

The queen pondered the question a moment and answered, "I have no idea."

The old woman responded, "You see, trees were planted by our forefathers for us to enjoy, and I am doing the same for those who will come along after me. How else can I repay my debt to those who lived before me?"

AUTHOR UNKNOWN

*P*eople once kept quiet about the disease of breast cancer, and the women who had it were like members of a secret club. Although things have changed, there is plenty of room for more change, because the winds of change are winds of hope.

CHAPTER SIX

The Longest Survivor

And we know that all things work together for good to them that love God, to them who are the called according to his purpose.

ROMANS 8:28 (KJV)

I HAD BEEN LOOKING FORWARD TO REKINDLING my friendship with Marcia Williams. Even though we had been friends for many years, Marcia had moved away, and I hadn't seen her for a long time. Our common bond was that she, too, was a wife and mother of two sons. When we ran into each other recently in the middle of downtown Little Rock, where more than 30,000 other women had gathered to run the annual Race for the Cure, we decided to catch up on one another's lives. She took time off from work to visit me at my studio, and over tall glasses of iced tea, we talked.

Marcia has been a breast cancer survivor for a long time. She is, in fact, the first person I actually knew to have breast cancer, but we had never really discussed it. She reminded me that when she found out she had breast cancer 35 years ago, nobody talked about it. She finally told me her story these many years later, because I finally asked.

Marcia's Story

Marcia was only 21 years old when she discovered a lump in her breast and went to her doctor for a checkup. At the time, mammograms weren't being used routinely. "I probably had one of the first mammograms in Arkansas," Marcia said. "I remember my doctor telling me about this new kind of X-ray that he wanted me to have. I sat in a chair with wheels on it and leaned forward over a cold table. The whole time I was afraid the chair was going to roll out from under me, because of the way they had me sitting. I was like a cat on a hot tin roof, holding on to that stainless steel table.

"After they took the X-ray, the doctor came in and told me, 'You have a great looking…(he smilingly paused) thumb.' I was holding on so hard trying to keep from sliding backwards in that rolling chair that my thumb was in the picture. I think that must have been a most primitive mammogram."

Following further investigation, the lump turned out to be cancerous. When Marcia's doctor told her that the cancer had metastasized, she had to ask him what that meant.

"Spread, Marcia," the doctor said gently. "It means it has spread into the surrounding tissues and is not contained inside the lump."

Though the terrible news stunned her, Marcia could not find anybody in her area to talk to who had been through breast cancer. Nobody was talking about it then. "Things were sort of whispered," Marcia recalled, "and my family was no different. I remember the first morning after surgery, I woke up at five still groggy from the anesthesia. My eyes opened and there stood my two uncles by my bed. These cattlemen farmers never bought flowers for their wives, but there they stood with a pot of blue plastic flowers. Somehow that was really funny to me…you just had to know Uncle Joe and Uncle Tom…and there by my bed they stood. I could feel all the bandages from my skin graft, so I knew the news was not good. By the looks on their faces, and the blue plastic flowers, I knew they were concerned. It was not even a pretty arrangement, but I kept those plastic flowers for years until they finally just got so old and brittle."

Marcia had undergone a radical mastectomy—the removal of breast, lymph nodes, muscles under the breast, and some of the surrounding fatty tissue. It was the most extensive surgery possible, and there was no follow-up treatment with chemotherapy or radiation. Her doctor provided a booklet on dos and don'ts, such as how to adjust your clothes after a mastectomy. That was the only information she had. There was no support group, no awareness group, and no other help.

Not only did the people around her not talk about the disease, Marcia noticed "almost an uncertain fear that I had something contagious. There might be a cancer germ. Back then, if we were invited to a potluck dinner, I was told I could bring paper plates."

At first I did not understand what Marcia was referring to, but she explained that people were being cautious not to eat any food she had prepared in her kitchen and with her hands...lest they catch her disease. If she wanted to bring something, she could bring paper plates—no food.

"I noticed that some of my family and friends would not even hug me," she said. "I think they were afraid of catching what I had. I was not too offended, because I understood that was just the way they were and they did not know any better. My grandmother had a different kind of cancer surgery, and my aunt would not hug her for the longest time, so I really was not too surprised."

Reach to Recovery

Marcia longed to find someone else who had gone through breast cancer. Arriving early one day to pick up a friend, she picked up the newspaper and saw a small ad about a training course for mastectomy patients. It was an answer to her prayer.

After responding to the ad, Marcia received a note from a nurse who'd had cancer and surgery when she was only 22. "We had a lot in common. The nurse was newly married like me and did not know anything about what she was going through with her mastectomy either. But she had gotten involved with the local chapter of the [American] Cancer Society."

Marcia and the nurse took the two-day training course together. There, they got to meet other cancer survivors. As it turned out, the woman who wrote the booklet Marcia's doctor had given her earlier was the same woman teaching the course, which was sponsored by a group called Reach to Recovery.

Marcia described the training session as dry and strict, like getting inducted into the Army. But what she learned in those two days marked the beginning of a lifelong volunteer project.

Marcia took her newfound courage and visited other mastectomy patients in the hospital after they had surgery. The nurse she'd befriended also became a volunteer, and the two shared their own stories of success with countless patients. Marcia and the nurse brought a ball for the patients to squeeze, showed them how to exercise, and most important of all, provided them an opportunity to visit with someone who had walked the same path. According to Marcia, the patients were more comfortable asking them questions than asking their own doctors.

Family Life

When her diagnosis came, Marcia was still a fairly new bride of three years. Her husband stood by her, never showing any signs of being bothered by the effects of her illness, and through it all was an "absolute saint," Marcia recalls.

"My surgery is from the old school of surgeons. My scar is very long; it goes from my neck all the way to my waist, with a terrible skin graft....[My husband] said that when he looks at that scar, he knows if it were not there, I would not be here."

Marcia's baby, Todd, was just two at the time. Because of her skin graft, she was not supposed to lift him, but she could change his diapers on the floor, and he was able to climb on the bed by himself.

Concerned about whether or not she would ever be able to have more children, Marcia would always bring up the subject on visits with her surgeon, and he would always say the same thing—"We'll talk about it in five years." Eventually, Marcia and her husband applied for a legal adoption and were approved. Then, five years and one month after her surgery, Marcia found out she was pregnant. "I hated to call the adoption agency and tell them I had a baby on the way, but things seemed to have a way of working out, and we were blessed with another baby boy."

When Clay was born, Marcia spent 11 days in the hospital. Afterward, her husband helped her go to the grocery store and run errands, because she was not supposed to drive. Like a rock, he was always there. Marcia's mother had died when she was 19, and since Marcia did not have any relatives living nearby, she found help from a neighbor as well as from several close friends. When no one was available to help, she took Todd along to her frequent doctor's visits, where he would sit and read. The nurses knew him by name and were really sweet to him.

Todd had no idea what his mother was going through until he grew on toward kindergarten age and gradually began to learn. Marcia described one incident when he was little. "He came into the bathroom when I was getting out of the shower, looked at my scar, and said, 'What happened to you?' I told him that was where Mama had surgery. He said, 'I'll go get you a Band-Aid.' That is what Mama did for him when he was hurt, and he was going to do the same for me."

Marcia and her husband tried to keep everything normal in their house; they did not dwell on the fact that she had cancer. As the years went by, Todd and Clay grew up not knowing any different. "One Sunday we were out for a drive and something on the radio came up about cancer. The announcer was referring to the fact that one in four people would get cancer of some type. All four of us were riding in the car, and after the announcement was over, Clay, spoke up and said, 'Mama, I am glad you got it over with for us.' I said, 'Well Clay, I am glad I did too.'"

A Second Round

As Marcia continued to go for regular visits to her doctor over the years, they both continued to worry about a recurrence. After 11 years, they came to the conclusion that a simple mastectomy on the other breast would put an end to the merry-go-round of worry for both of them. As it turned out, a small tumor found during that surgery was malignant too, but the good news was that it was contained. "The second time I had breast cancer, it was not related to the first time nor was it a recurrence. It was a totally different type of cancer. My doctor told me it had nothing to do with the first cancer."

Sitting in my studio, Marcia shared with me her reflections of how times have changed. "Thirty-five years ago, they did not do chemotherapy or radiation treatments…or if they did, it was very rare. Especially the chemo treatments were rare, and if they did use them, it was when a patient was in her final stages of the disease. It was not used as a preventive treatment; it just helped to prolong a life. Now, as a precautionary measure, radiation and chemotherapy are often both used."

When Marcia went through surgery for the second time, she found the experience to be much easier than the first. "Of course, I was not thrilled about having to take radiation and chemotherapy," she said, "but my husband, friends, and my church were always there for me. I can actually say that the radiation and the chemo treatments were all really good experiences. Everybody that I came in contact with was so nice, especially the nurses in radiation."

Marcia noted that she always felt flustered while getting dressed in one of the little rooms after a treatment. The rooms had no mirrors, and she had to go down the hall to comb her hair and put on her lipstick. "I mentioned to the nurses that a little mirror hung in the room sure would be nice," she said. "On a return visit just two days later, I could hardly believe the full-length mirrors that had been immediately installed in each room. We were all growing, making changes, and getting through this together."

But like many of the women I interviewed, Marcia was hit hard by the loss of her hair. "When I had the second mastectomy and was losing my hair because of the chemo, I was just devastated," she said. "Even though I knew my hair would come back, it was the fact that my hair was coming out by the handfuls that upset me. I would have to get the vacuum cleaner out after brushing my hair. I asked my husband last night what the worst part was about all of this, and he said, 'Losing your hair. And it did not bother me, but I knew it upset you so much.'"

Even in her years of volunteering, Marcia said she found it awkward to talk about hair loss with a new cancer patient. "You can't tell them that your hair will grow back and everything will be okay," she said. But having gone through hair loss herself, she could offer comfort when it was needed.

Risk Factors

Humor helped Marcia to keep things in perspective. Marcia remembers teasing one patient that she worked with about her own cancer being caused by the cod liver oil. "No, I'm just kidding," Marcia said. Explaining that when she was a little girl, she'd been given a spoonful of cod liver oil every time she was sick. Marcia told the patient, "I just decided anything that tastes that bad cannot be good for you. Oh! That stuff was awful."

The causes of breast cancer are something Marcia and I both have puzzled over, and knowing the risk factors sometimes makes the disease seem even more of a mystery. According to the Memorial Sloan-Kettering Cancer Center in New York, 70 percent of the women who develop breast cancer have no known risk factors such as alcohol use, smoking, lack of exercise, or a family history of the disease.

I asked Marcia if she had any notion of what caused her breast cancer at such a young age. She had been searching for an answer, she said, and had concluded that being from a little Southern farming town probably contributed to the cause. The surrounding farms—with their open ditches and reservoirs of standing water for rice crops—were an excellent breeding ground for mosquitoes. To control the mosquitoes, the town sprayed. Trucks passed up and down the streets, blanketing the town with a heavy fog of DDT, a pesticide since banned in this country.

"They just sprayed the streets good with that stuff," Marcia remembered. "They even used it in the house. My aunt had a little red wool Oriental rug that I used to play dolls on. The rug was sprayed with DDT to keep out the moths. I can remember getting sick, and I even broke out into a rash."

Educating Others

Marcia talked about how awkward her breast cancer was for other people to relate to. People did not know what to say and quite often would put their foot right in their mouth. "I was at the State Fair and ran into a friend that I had not seen in a long time. The lady looked surprised to see me. She proceeded to greet me, 'Marcia, I hear you are doing so bad.'" Marcia told her she thought she was doing all right. The friend reversed her statement and told Marcia she did *not* look so bad. That really bothered Marcia because it made her feel concerned. She asked her husband, "Is there something you are not telling me?"

Even with the best of intentions, people were often at a loss. "People cannot just look at you and see that you have breast cancer," Marcia said. "That is a characteristic of breast cancer— a person does not *look* sick....I think the gift of humor probably got me through a lot back then."

But sometimes people were simply insensitive. "Once in a while," Marcia recalled, "there was something that slapped me in the face, like the time I needed a swim suit. Remember that this was before the days of having specialty stores or even areas within a store for mastectomy patients. I needed a swimsuit that came up high on the chest to hide my scar. I needed a swimsuit that was contoured to stay in place and did not fall forward. I had looked and looked and looked. One day I went into one of the finest and most expensive little dress shops in our town thinking they might have what I needed. I found the swimsuits on the rack, and a pushy little saleslady who apparently worked on commission asked if she could help me. I told her what I was looking for, and she kept pulling out low-cut swimsuits, one after another. I tried on several, and, of course, none of them worked. Finally I told her that I had a scar I was trying to cover up, which came up to my collarbone. She said I was just going to have to wear a T-shirt over my swimsuit. I didn't cry, but I sure wanted to."

Marcia left the store and went into one down the street, where she spotted a rack of swimsuits near the front door. The first swimsuit she saw worked fine. "I was so tempted to go back and show that saleslady what I found. Thinking back, I know that she probably did not mean anything by what she said. She was insensitive to my situation, but probably had no idea I was offended."

To Them that Love God

One of the nicest things anyone ever did for Marcia was when the wife of her husband's boss took the time to write Marcia a four-page letter. Rather elderly, the woman was unable to visit Marcia. "Through the shaky penmanship, I could tell she wanted to encourage me and give me hope," Marcia said. "In her letter she lifted up the scripture verse of Romans 8:28: *And we know that all things work together for good to those who love God, to those who are the called according to His purpose.* That scripture lifted my spirits and nourished my soul. I keep that scripture on the tip of my tongue, and always in my heart....She knew my mother was not living, and I just felt like she was such a special friend for feeding me that scripture. I have kept and treasured her letter all these years."

Her walk with God brought peace and perspective to Marcia's battle with breast cancer. She was told that with breast cancer, she would pass through different mental stages— "anger, denial, depression...and I don't remember the rest," Marcia said. "The most important thing is that I do not remember being angry. I look back and wonder if I missed out on a phase or something, but I don't ever remember getting angry. For one thing, who would I get mad at? I was not mad at God, because I knew he did not cause this. I can remember getting mad at someone over something they said, like the lady who tried to sell me a swimsuit. Sometimes I am sad, because I lost my mother at 19, and I wish my mother were here with me. But then I think, well, maybe it is a good thing Mother was not around all this. Maybe it is best she did not know."

Marcia doesn't remember ever getting depressed either. Nor did she get angry with the aunt who would not hug her anymore. "I understood her uneducated ways," she said. "As the years went by, I remember the day I knew I was going to be all right. It was the day my aunt hugged me. I remember thinking: She must think I am all right."

Marcia cried over her hair loss, but when she looks back, she said, she doesn't think she ever had much to cry about. "Although what was the likelihood that I would have breast cancer at the young age of 21?"

When she considers her overall experience, she sees "so much good has come out of this experience that never would have happened otherwise."

In her volunteer work, Marcia often has the opportunity to encourage other cancer patients. "It seems odd to tell a new cancer patient that they will have some of the best experiences of their life," she said, "but I do. I tell them that, even though they might not understand right away that good things will come out of all this, they will become a much better person because of it. Some patients I have visited through the years understood this, and some could not even imagine it. I always let them know from my experience and others' who have been through the same, that each new day will be better than the day before."

Keeping a Good Outlook

Marcia sometimes wonders why she got a completely unrelated second cancer. But there were good things that came out of that, too, she said, and she thinks she knows the answer to her question of why.

"In the Reach to Recovery program that I volunteered in, we needed a volunteer who had been through radiation and chemotherapy treatments....Our group tries to match up patients with a volunteer who has the most in common whether it be age, occupation, or treatment. Since I was the one who had first been through both, the volunteer we needed was me. I was able to share my successful experience of chemo and radiation all while raising two young children and with a husband at work every day."

Today, Marcia tells new cancer patients that breast cancer is certainly not a death sentence. She calls herself "living proof." And while the fact of having breast cancer is hard to understand in the beginning, Marcia says, "In some strange way, it can be a gift." So has it been in her life. She believes that "Even in the absolute worst case of breast cancer in the final stages, the gift is time—time to tell your family and those closest all the things you need to say. It is not like a tragic car accident, where death is immediate and there is no time to tell someone you love him or her."

Marcia appreciates that she was given a wakeup call. Not everybody is given the chance to realize what is really important in the larger scheme of things, she said. "Simply seeing my boys grow up is what was important to me. I gained a totally new perspective about what is trivial and what is really important."

A Whole New Light of Appreciation

Letting certain people in her life know what they have done for her has been a real gift also—the gift of being allowed to show appreciation. But likewise, she has also been given the gift of being appreciated.

Her church offered suggestions for a letter-writing program, meant to encourage people to write individuals who had made an impression on them in order to let them know it. Marcia recalls, "My friend Charlene wrote me a letter on how much she admired what I had been through, and the courage with which I handled it. I was just getting by with God's help, as graceful as I could, because I knew I was in his hands, and he was my strength. I did not see myself as courageous but I guess she did, and that handwritten letter meant so much. It truly does take a village to raise a child, and I am living proof, because without my church, my family, and my friends, I would not be the same. And I am a better person because of it all."

Marcia said she is not alone in making such a statement. Through her years of volunteering and talking to other cancer patients, they, too, have said they are better persons for having cancer…wiser, stronger, more appreciative, and with a much deeper faith. "Even after all these years, sunrises are more glorious, sunsets are more colorful, changing leaves are more intense, and I just thank God for the gift of another day. I remember a friend telling me, 'Today is our gift from God, that is why we call it the present.'"

Sharing from her own experience, Marcia always tells a new cancer patient that they will notice and appreciate things like never before. "We don't seem to take things for granted," she said. "I remember on my way home from the hospital, it was

September, and I thought that the grass was oh so green. Well, in looking back all those years, the grass could not have been very green at all, because September is one of the driest and can be one of the hottest months we have here in the South. It was actually the time of the year when the grass starts turning brown, but I thought the grass was so green. Little things are just seen in a whole new light of appreciation."

Out in the Open

Now that there's so much information out in the open, new cancer patients will sometimes go and buy every book on the shelf. Marcia did that too. It even got to the point that if there were a new magazine lying around the house, her husband would say, "What's it got in it about breast cancer?" Standing in line at the grocery store, the magazine headlines about breast cancer seemed to jump out at her, all the way from *Good Housekeeping* to the *National Enquirer.*

"Through the years, I have watched even the magazine topics change," Marcia commented. "Thank goodness for the high profile people who shared their stories, such as Betty Ford, Nancy Reagan, Happy Rockefeller, and Sandra Day O'Connor. Before first lady Betty Ford told her story of surviving breast cancer, none of the magazines would even publish articles of information on breast cancer, much less diagrams of how to do a breast self-exam."

What Marcia said was all too true. My research showed that countless other celebrity women faced this disease but apparently chose not to talk about it. On an even sadder note, no one was ready to listen. I discovered that breast cancer has been recognized as far back as 1523 in Italy. Some historians and physicians believe that Michelangelo's sculpture *Night,* of a reclining, muscular woman accurately reproduced in stone by the master himself, reveals the likelihood of her having an advanced stage of breast cancer. Although no one can actually prove the case of Michelangelo's sculpture representing a breast cancer sufferer, it is very suggestive.

Thirty-five years ago, Marcia was surprised when people almost came out of the bushes to tell her that they'd had breast surgery too. It was almost like a secret club, she recalls. She got letters from ladies who had been through breast surgery years ago and did not tell a soul, as if they were embarrassed and had something to hide. Now women are talking out in the open, in part because of the courageous women who had a voice and an audience of reporters. And in part because of extraordinary housewives like Marcia, who likewise had a voice and chose not only to speak about their personal experience of having breast cancer, but also to reach out to other women facing the same struggle.

Nonetheless, it took too many years for people to focus national and international attention on what was happening to women. Breast cancer strikes in all countries, among all nationalities, all ages of women, and all colors, Marcia pointed out. While the world has only recently brought this into focus, breast cancer has been a reality in the lives of Marcia's family for 35 years and is something they all learned to live with and deal with openly.

"My son is now 37, and he has not known his mother any other way," Marcia said. "We don't ever talk about it now, unless the subject comes up on its own. He has had business acquaintances who have had wives, sisters, or mothers diagnosed with breast cancer, and he will tell them we have been through all that. He will offer his phone number if they need it, and say, 'Call me.'

"As time goes by I think the boys have come to realize how lucky they were to have their mother, even with what we all went through. But that brings me to the importance of early detection, especially by having an annual mammogram. Sometimes I get on my soapbox and warn young women not to let their doctors put off a lump they find because they are young.

Things would be quite different if I had put off going to the doctor, or he had put off his concern."

Winds of Hope

Times have changed. People are more aware and knowledgeable about breast cancer. But there is still plenty of room for more change, and the winds of change are winds of hope.

Not only does the woman with breast cancer need educational materials, but also the support teams that surround those wives, sisters, mothers, and daughters need to be educated too. Getting this information out in the open to support patients and their circle of friends and family is most important. Likewise, more women need to find out about prevention and early detection. We are all still learning about the disease, and we are learning to open up our minds and hearts as well.

For Marcia, who has seen so much change in the knowledge and treatment of cancer in her lifetime, the amount of change is "almost unreal." The very first Race for the Cure was just a couple of days before her birthday. All Marcia's friends were busy or not interested, so she ended up going to the race by herself. "I was so amazed that even at the very first Race for the Cure there were several thousand participants," she said, "and I thought to myself, *what a wonderful birthday*. I was so moved by just coming to the race, because I visibly saw I was not alone. All these people were trying to do something about breast cancer and did not have to hide to talk about it."

The annual fall Race is now several years old, and Marcia and I both are continually amazed at the turnout of survivors, and supporters as the race numbers continue to grow each year.

Marcia recalls, "The first year that I walked the race, I ran into a woman I had counseled in the hospital following her mastectomy. She had been a schoolteacher where my son had gone to high school, so as we caught up on the past we ended up walking the 5K together. Thus began a yearly tradition, which we have continued through the years, meeting on race day and walking together."

This year, Marcia attended the annual survivors luncheon that was held immediately following the race. She and her schoolteacher walking-buddy slipped in late to get seated. "We were asked by several women that we did not know to sit at a table close to the front," Marcia said. "We quietly took our seats, because the speaker had already started the program. I saw that the woman to my right must have taken chemo, because she wore a cap that hid the fact that her hair was gone. I was not able to say anything to her, because the speaker was talking. The speaker was calling attention to the longest survivors in attendance at the race day luncheon. Five-year survivors stood, ten-year survivors stood, 20-year survivors stood, 30-year survivors stood. But when it came to 35 years, I was the only one standing. I was recognized as being the longest survivor of breast cancer in the race.

"As I sat back in my chair, this stranger with her cap on reached over and hugged me. I was so worried about being late that I had not given a thought to where I would sit. Apparently, God knew exactly where I needed to be seated, because this woman was a new cancer patient who needed to see what was possible. I will never know her name, but I will never forget her."

I know Marcia does not think of herself as being a pillar of strength, but to the lady sitting next to her, she was. Marcia told me: "She needed a hug, and God put me there to give it to her. I wish I could have told her how I got my strength from my faith in God, my family, and my friends."

Practice tenderhearted mercy and kindness to others.…
Be gentle and ready to forgive
Never hold any grudges.…
Most of all let love guide your life.
COLOSSIANS 3:12-14 (TLB)

My Cup Runneth Over

My afternoon treat of Marcia's visit was coming to an end. She was meeting her husband and some friends for dinner, but she still had more to share. This woman who'd gone through two separate battles with breast cancer, the longest living survivor in the Race, wanted to tell me about her cup.

"Somehow I always saw my glass as being full of water," she said, "and when something is full you need to share it because there is too much. I was blessed with a wonderful husband and two sons that God gave me, and I still continue to drink from a saucer because my cup has overflowed. I know in my heart what let me gracefully walk through all of this, because at the time I did not realize how difficult the journey really was. My life was changed forever, and for the better, 35 years ago in that doctor's office. With God's gifts of faith, family, and friends, my sadness and sorrows were divided, and my joys were yet multiplied."

As I stood up to take Marcia's empty iced-tea glass and walk her to the door, we hugged. Marcia turned to me and said, "Funny thing. I attended my twenty-fifth high school reunion and was voted 'The Least Most Changed.'"

Breast cancer is not a death sentence. It can be a gift, a wake-up call. Not everyone is given the chance to realize what truly matters in the scheme of things. Breast cancer offers perspective between what is trivial, and what is really important. It gives you time to let people know how much you really love them.

When my time is up and I stand before my maker,
I'd like to be able to say,
God, I don't have one ounce
of talent, love, compassion or energy left.
I used every gift you gave me.

Today is not yesterday—we change.
How then can our works and thoughts,
If they are always to be the fittest,
Continue always the same.
Change indeed is painful, yet ever needful;
And if memory have its force and worth,
So also has hope.

THOMAS CARLYLE

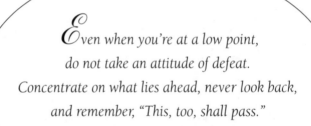

*Even when you're at a low point,
do not take an attitude of defeat.
Concentrate on what lies ahead, never look back,
and remember, "This, too, shall pass."*

CHAPTER SEVEN

This, Too, Shall Pass

> It is said an Eastern monarch once charged his
> wise men to invent him a sentence to be ever in
> view, and which should be true and appropriate in
> all times and situations. They presented him the
> words: "And this, too, shall pass away." How much
> it expresses! How chastening in the hour of pride!
> How consoling in the depths of affliction!
>
> ABRAHAM LINCOLN

THROUGH THE YEARS, I HAVE ALWAYS ENJOYED the witty comments
from syndicated columnist, speaker, and award-winning writer
Maryln Schwartz. Headquartered in Dallas, Texas, Maryln is
probably best known for her book that appeared on the *New
York Times* bestseller list, *A Southern Belle Primer*. It is a book
that is honest, humorous, and true to her style of writing, in
which Maryln takes a no-holds-barred look at Southern
women along with their traditions and their manners.

Maryln gives us a laugh when she writes in her books and
columns about the art of being Southern. Her close-to-the-
bone humor tackles big hair, silverware patterns, finger bowls,
the Junior League, wedding protocol, sorority choices, and the
art of choosing a proper name for a daughter.

Maryln is often asked, just what is the South? Her charming answer meanders through a series of questions and snappy comments. Is Texas too southwestern? Is Virginia too East Coast? Traditionally, the South is defined by the states that seceded from the Union during the Civil War—Texas, Arkansas, Louisiana, Tennessee, Mississippi, Alabama, Georgia, Florida, South Carolina, North Carolina, and Virginia—as well as Kentucky as a border state.

But Maryln says there is a much easier way of deciding. "Just go to any 'home cooking' restaurant in any town you're visiting. If the menu lists macaroni and cheese as a vegetable— you know you are in the South."

When I spoke with Maryln, this "steel magnolia" talked about a subject of more serious note, her experience with having breast cancer. I called her one morning, and she was delighted to share her story. I was not surprised by the positive attitude she displayed about her experience, but I was surprised by some of the details.

"Having breast cancer is not the worst thing that has ever happened to me," Maryln told me. "Actually, some good things have come out of this. I even think it has improved my writing. It has freed me up. I can just let loose and write."

Let loose and write? I thought that is what Maryln had done all along. Having always admired Maryln as someone who spoke freely, I sat back to listen. If Maryln was now even freer in expressing how she sees the world, I knew she was not going to mince words when it came to talking about her breast cancer.

Like Murphy Brown

Delightful, witty, and often outrageous, Maryln compared herself to the television character Murphy Brown, whose first show of that season had a familiar scenario for women— nervously awaiting the news of a mammogram.

For thousands of women each year, this is not just TV, Maryln emphasized. That particular episode was about all the women who had traveled this path. "Murphy Brown got breast cancer, and so did I," she said. "Through tears and laughter, watching the episode not only gave me strength, it made me laugh. I was late for my mammogram. So was Murphy. Both of us assumed we had a press pass to life. How could anything be wrong with us? We wrote about crises, we didn't involve ourselves in them."

Like other women with whom I talked, Marlyn did not believe this could happen to her. She'd been one of those people who were really busy, and she did not get her mammogram on time.

"If anybody wonders what it feels like to sit in that room waiting to hear the results, and you think, *maybe I have this stuff, and I might have put it off.* Well, I'll tell you what you feel like," Maryln said. "You feel like you were stupid, and you almost killed yourself. And if that makes people upset, well good. Breast cancer is so treatable. I always wondered how I'd feel if I waited too long and found out the mammogram wasn't okay…well, I got to find out. I felt like a fool. It was so stupid, so unnecessary."

One of the characters on the Murphy Brown show said she did not need a mammogram because breast cancer did not run in her family. Breast cancer did not run in Maryln's family either. Maryln wasn't years late for the mammogram, just months. But those eight months almost cost Maryln her life.

As busy as she was, when she did have a break from her work, she chose to do other things rather than go in for her mammogram. Maryln knew other women who practiced the same kind of avoidance. "One day I had some time and thought about getting the mammogram. Instead I chose to clean out my closet. Only the thought of a mammogram could make me clean out my closet. I know one woman who canceled her mammogram because she heard the lines were short on weekdays to see *Evita*. She could always get a mammogram, but *Evita* was a tough ticket."

While Maryln uses humor to help maintain her positive attitude, she does not allow humor to detract from her message. "If hearing all this makes you uncomfortable," she said, "it should. Get that mammogram. Nothing is worse than realizing you might have lessened your odds."

Maryln praised her doctors, who were truthful in all that they said. One of them advised her, "Never look back." In Maryln's situation, she might easily have become stuck in the notion that she should have acted differently or done something sooner, because by the time her cancer was detected and treated, it was already advanced.

"I had stage three, which is bad," she reported. "It was a huge tumor. Stage four is the last, and it was still not a death sentence. My doctor was tough, realistic, and sensitive to my feelings. I took his advice and just concentrated on what lay ahead."

During one intimate conversation with her doctor, Maryln was told, "This is not to say nothing can be done, and I won't say that I am not worried about you. I just want you to gather up every bit of strength and spirituality, because we are going to fight this."

Scared to ask in a direct manner what her odds were, Maryln instead put it this way to her doctor: "I am redoing my house and I'm putting in long-wearing carpet. It's very expensive. Is there any reason I shouldn't choose the long-wearing?"

After a heart-stopping pause, her doctor smiled and said, "Maryln, go for the plush." In a similar television episode, Murphy Brown told her doctor, "If I buy green bananas, I just want to know if I am going to be around to see them ripen."

You Have Such a Good Chance

Maryln did not begin treatment with surgery. She and her doctors chose chemotherapy first, hoping to shrink the tumor before the mastectomy.

"Chemotherapy!" Maryln exclaimed. "The very word was terror. I had heard all the stories. I thought even if I lived, the quality of life would be horrible. Well, let me tell you, I had an easy time with chemotherapy."

Her chemo treatments made her tired, but Maryln was able to bring all her work home with her and never missed writing one of her daily columns. "Actually, one of the nicest things to come out of all this is the fact that I decided I liked working at home," she told me. "I go into the newspaper office once or twice a week or so, but I can get more done if I stay here at home."

Maryln approached the vicissitudes of chemotherapy with her characteristic humor and positive attitude. "I lost my hair," she said, "but that was not the worst thing. It wasn't horrible, because I knew it was coming out. I went out and bought a wig. There are some wonderful wigs, and *every* day was a good hair day. It was fabulous. You are going to live, and your hair will come back. So what...in the meantime you can have something that makes you look wonderful.

"People gathered round and looked miserable for me. I remember thinking, '*They are even dividing up my jewelry.*'"

One person asked Maryln, not too subtly, how one goes about applying to write a column for the newspaper. "The position is not open," Maryln informed her. "From that day, I was determined I would do whatever it takes, and *live*. The chemotherapy turned out to be a big surprise. I was mentally prepared to be sick, and I just thought, *This, too, shall pass.*"

Maryln took every chemo that you can have, and it was not a terrible thing. She lauded new developments in the world of chemotherapy, wonderful medicines that keep most people from being nauseated. She did not experience terrible vomiting. She got very, very tired but never had to stop any of her activities.

Maryln told me, in fact, that she developed great calm as she fought her way through. "It seems like you spend your life worrying that the worst is going to happen," she said. "And then the worst does happen. I found out that it was not the worst."

When Maryln came home from her first chemotherapy treatment, a friend came to stay with her. Marilyn described her reaction to the treatment. "I rested on the couch, and he brought dinner," Maryln reported. "We waited. We ate dinner and I sat on the couch. We waited. We watched the news and we waited. My friend was hovering, and finally I said, 'I feel fine. Let's go to the movies.' And that was a shock. I was really prepared for terrible things.

"Now, I am not saying it did not make me tired. Of course it did. It was just not horrible. I could work from home and never had to stop writing my column. Even when I was at a low point, I would choose to say, 'This, too, shall pass.'"

Maryln's column for the *Dallas Morning News* usually focuses on politics, sports, and whatever new is happening in the world. Maryln was between treatments when the newspaper asked her to travel to Washington and write about the presidential inauguration. After a few days in Washington, Maryln wrote to her doctor on a postcard: "The chill factor is ten below zero. It is so crowded and there's no place to sit at the ball. It takes you an hour to walk two feet and there is nothing to eat at the ball. You can't get a reservation at a restaurant, and there are no cabs to be had. All in all, chemotherapy is easier."

Maryln's characteristic humor has clearly been a morale booster and a means for helping her survive. "I am not trying to make light of chemotherapy," Maryln said. "I want anyone going through this to think of it as something positive. I do not want anyone to get breast cancer. But if it is there, it is not the horror story it used to be. If you get to the doctor and get the treatments, you have such a good chance…even me, who was a stage three. I know that it is a serious procedure that affects people in different ways. I was lucky. I tolerated it extremely well. But even people who had problems with chemotherapy did not report horror stories. Mostly, they said they were very,

very tired for a few days after the treatments. Others said it was like getting the flu."

As resilient as Maryln proved to be, the effects of chemotherapy did present difficult surprises. "The only thing I wasn't prepared for, because nobody told me, was about losing my eyebrows and eyelashes," she said. "Maybe some don't, but I did. So one morning I got up and looked in the mirror and did not have any eyelashes or eyebrows. I thought I had prepared myself for everything, and this was a silly little thing…but I burst into tears. Then I realized that it was not just the eyelashes—my tears had built up about everything. I cried for about five minutes, washed my face, put on some eyeliner, and brushed on some eyebrows with makeup. Not one person ever knew it. It was just one of those silly little things. I think it is extra important to put on your makeup and just feel good about yourself looking into that mirror. I did pay more attention to putting on my makeup, because it made me feel good."

Thankful for Something to Do

Everyone who goes on this journey needs something to help them get through it. Whether its friends, family, support groups, church, or Scripture, every woman suffering from breast cancer needs something outside herself to look to.

When I asked Maryln how she managed to get through all this, she told me she saw her work as a blessing. "I was so lucky to be a writer, and I could write from home. But the reason is *not* that I was so devoted; it was because I was thankful for something to do. I decided I would rather have people say, 'Isn't she brave?' instead of 'She does nothing but whine.'"

Maryln is the kind of woman who likes to be occupied. She likes to get up and go places, put on her makeup, and pay attention to how she looks. Her attitude toward her wig was not "how horrible it is I have to wear a wig," but rather, "I have the most glorious hair." Getting up and going places, working on her newspaper column, putting on her makeup and so forth helped Maryln to feel good about herself.

"I knew inside me that it was really Estee Lauder on the outside, but so what," Maryln commented. "I don't know if that is courage, but you just have to be in charge of yourself."

The journey through breast cancer is not all terrible, Maryln emphasized. Indeed, she found much to be grateful for. "My friends were so wonderful, it was just unbelievable…and that in itself was a wonderful thing to happen. I found out that I had strength that I did not know I could have. I learned to trust…I learned to trust in myself. You just have to get up and do it. Now there were some days that I would get a good book, get in the bed, and pull the covers over my head, but *Get Over It*! Move on!"

Her strength also came through faith, but Maryln emphasized that you have to put faith in yourself, too. Maryln's faith is very personal. "I could not just say that I will put this in someone else's hands and give up. You can use prayer, you use your friends, and I put my faith in all these things, but I knew I had to be the one to do the work. We are granted choices. We can choose to have a good attitude, or we can choose to have a bad attitude. I told myself I was going to beat this. I chose to have a good attitude."

Although Maryln did gather strength from faith and friends, for her the bottom line was: "*I* had to be the one willing to do the work. My attitude relaxed as I just accepted the things I would have to do. And when the going got rough, I would just remember the promise, *This, too, shall pass.*"

Maryln did not undergo a mastectomy until three months after the discovery of her cancer. "I hid my nervousness in strange ways," she told me. "The night before surgery, a friend came over with dinner…and I was madly cleaning my house!"

When her friend demanded to know what she was doing, Maryln answered, "Straightening up." Her friend reminded her, "You are having major surgery in the morning. Why are you doing that now?"

Maryln said to him, "Well, people will be coming over when I get back from the hospital. My mother would die if she thought the place was a mess."

Her friend answered her, "Maryln, your mother is dead. Stop that right now."

Being Selective About Doctors

Blessed by good friendships, Maryln also was blessed by the skill of her surgeon. After she had her mastectomy, the day came when they took off the bandages. This is sometimes a frightening time, because a woman will be seeing her chest for the first time after her breast has been removed. Maryln was prepared. "I just wanted to live," she said.

Her doctor helped with the transition, supporting her emotionally and psychologically, reinforcing the positive. Maryln described the scene: "He stood there, and he kind of put his arm around me from behind while the nurse was taking off my bandages. He said, 'Now Maryln, I want you to know that to me it is beautiful, because it is good healthy tissue.' I remember thinking, 'Now wasn't that a wonderful thing to say.'"

Women who are dealing with breast cancer need to be selective about their doctors, Maryln stressed. "If you are with one you don't like, who is not talking to you or who makes you feel uncomfortable, go to another one. Having a wonderful breast surgeon and a wonderful oncologist was so comforting to me. I felt like they provided me with a good foundation, because there are frightening times when you need someone to talk to that you can trust."

Handling it Your Own Way

Maryln, who wanted to do everything possible to combat the cancer, went through her regular series of chemotherapy and then took another one. Then she underwent radiation. "None of it was hard," she said. "Nothing about it was awful."

Every woman has to handle treatment in her own way, and for many women, a support group is highly beneficial. But Maryln did not choose that course. Once she had finished treatment, she decided she was not going to live her life as if breast cancer were the point of her life. "Something happened to me," she said, "and I did all I could do to take care of it. I don't make it a huge part of my life…I just go on with life."

Maryln did find a support group among the people she knew. She surrounded herself with good friends and positive people. Many women may not be so lucky, she said, especially in the rural countryside. But breast cancer is so prevalent, there will likely be somebody nearby who has gone through this.

"Years ago we did not talk about it, and that is what's so important about the groups that have formed," she said. Although she did not feel the need to attend a support group per se, she emphasized that each cancer patient must make her own decision about what is best for her.

Maryln even looked outside the area in which she lived for guidance, contacting the Komen Foundation. "I was well aware of the Komen Breast Cancer Awareness Foundation that Nancy Brinker started in memory of her sister," Maryln said. "Friends helped me get through this and steered me in the right direction."

Maryln found her support not in groups, but individually and personally, through humor and friendship. Not everyone can see humor in such a situation, but humor was particularly important to Maryln. She felt blessed by the gift of laughter that her friends helped bring to her life during this experience. "I never lost my sense of humor through all of this. I think laughing is so good…it releases those endorphins. You just can't feel sorry for yourself. Instead of saying, 'Why did this happen to me?' Say: 'Isn't this wonderful? I am surviving.'"

When Maryln had surgery, the hospital was full. She spent only two days there, during which she shared a room with a lovely woman who was a grandmother and had just had painful colon cancer surgery. "She was given a morphine pump to relieve the pain," Maryln said. "But she rarely used it."

The woman told Maryln, "I don't want to risk the chance of getting addicted. I can stand the pain for a little while."

While they were talking, they were also watching television. Another football player had been suspended for using drugs. "His excuse was he just needed it to help him get through the pain," Maryln said.

"I smiled at that tough, strong grandmother and will always remember her. If she could do it, I bet a young, big, strong football player could too."

You Know You Are Alive

Of all the passions, fear weakens judgement most.
CARDINAL DE RETZ

Maryln ended our conversation by telling me she was working on a deadline for her column and had to be downtown by ten o'clock that morning. I thanked her for sharing her story.

Once again Maryln emphasized the positive. "Having breast cancer is not horrible," she said. "There is reconstruction that is incredible. You know you are alive." That knowledge set her free, she said. Knowing she was alive helped her combat her fear. "I am not as scared as I used to be. I know now what is really important. Having breast cancer has actually helped my writing, and I have this new attitude of being a bit bolder. If anything, this whole experience has taught me the wisdom of that old adage, 'Life is what happens while you are planning for something else.' You never know what is in store for you. And there is a bright side. The worst has happened to me, and I made it through."

Maryln's attitude can be an inspiration to every woman. She made the mistake of putting off her mammogram, but she did not take an attitude of defeat. Putting off the mammogram does not necessarily mean that it is all over. It doesn't mean you just throw your hands up in the air and say, "I quit," and live off that excuse. Turn that mistake into a springboard for becoming a successful survivor. As Maryln says, "Just go get the mammogram."

Be selective about your doctors. If you are with one you do not like, who is not talking to you or who makes you uncomfortable, go to another one.

Your character is
the result of your conduct.

ARISTOTLE

*G*od brings us to our knees when
we least expect it. By opening our hearts to others,
by learning to receive their blessings and prayers,
we also learn how to serve. God does not give all
the answers at once, but the answers are there.

CHAPTER EIGHT

Painting Sisterhood

*You built no great cathedrals
That centuries applaud,
But with a grace exquisite
Your life cathedraled God.*

THOMAS FESSENDEN

PLANNING TO WRITE SOME THANK-YOU NOTES, I picked up a box of cards at a gift store not too long ago. The cards caught my eye because of the beautiful images of three women, all wearing hats. I thought the cards were pretty, and I was in a hurry. Like so many other women who have happened across these cards, little did I know how special those cards would come to be.

After bringing the cards home, I opened one, intent on writing to a friend of mine who had surprised me by sending flowers on my birthday. But before I began to write, the note on the back of the card caught my attention.

"*About the Artist,*" I read from across the top. "*Vicki Kovaleski is a watercolorist in Little Rock, Arkansas. As an artist, her theme is to tell stories in her paintings—many of which are personal. As a woman fighting breast cancer, Vicki tells us about her experiences with the healing power of sisterhood in her latest work, The Sisterhood Series.*"

A picture is worth a thousand words, we've all been told, and as I inspected the cards more closely, I noticed that each of the cards in the little white box truly did tell a story.

Our paths have recently crossed through business, and now Vicki Kovaleski is my friend. Since we live in the same city, I went by her studio for a brief visit to ask about her work and her personal experience with breast cancer.

Vicki graciously showed me some of the commissions she was working on, including a patriotic tribute to the New York firemen and policemen who were involved in rescue efforts after the September 2001 terrorist attack on the World Trade Center. I saw framed magazine covers that featured her artwork displayed on the wall. But as I walked through her sunlit studio, it was very obvious to me that Vicki's heart is in the portraits of women wearing colorful hats, similar to the cards I bought at that gift store.

I sat on an overstuffed sofa, the sun warming my shoulders, as Vicki shared with me her story of how the cards came to be.

Sisterhood Series

"I had no idea that I would have a card company, because all I wanted to do was paint," she said. "When I was diagnosed with breast cancer, my therapy was that I just had to paint. I don't think God gives you all the answers at once, because if he did, I might run! When I had a good day, I just needed to paint. I did not know what I was going to do with the pictures. I just knew that I needed to paint. I felt like I was doing what God wanted me to do for the moment. Paint!"

Vicki explained that when she was first diagnosed, her doctor recommended that she talk to someone who had been through the same disease she had. "I am a very private person," she told me. "I did not want to talk to anybody, but the doctor persisted and said he would have a lady named Evelyn call me if I would give him permission."

Evelyn called and asked Vicki if she thought it would help to see what a mastectomy reconstruction looked like. As it turned out, Vicki realized that she and Evelyn had much in common. They were even members of the same church, although their church was so large they had never met. The two set a date and time to meet, and when Vicki went to see her, Evelyn quickly lifted up her shirt without embarrassment and said, "This is it!" Pleasantly stunned, Vicki said she thought, *I can live with that.*

After an awkward first meeting, the two ladies became dear friends. Since Evelyn had gone through her mastectomy and reconstruction just three weeks earlier, she knew how important it was to have a friend go along with you for the hours and hours of lab work.

"Evelyn would not let me go alone to the tests and scans," Vicki reported. "It was the first time in my life that I felt I was not human anymore. I was a number on a wristband. It was a time of just waiting for this test and that test. Having Evelyn there with me was so nice, just to have another set of ears to hear what the doctors said, because I think I sort of went into shock. When the news is not good, it helps to have somebody there with you when you go up and down on that roller coaster ride. Just her being there with me was priceless."

Only three weeks postoperative herself, Evelyn nonetheless sat there with Vicki through it all. "We had plenty of time to think," Vicki commented. "We talked about chemotherapy and losing our hair. She had not started her chemo yet but was told she would probably be losing her hair."

Vicki organized a "Hat Day" party, inviting not only Evelyn, but also another friend who was going through chemotherapy, and a photographer friend to take pictures. The three ladies were photographed trying on hats.

"We tried to have fun trying on hats that day," Vicki remembered, "but in retrospect, we were all very scared of the coming treatment and the possibility of losing our hair. With those photographs, I began to paint. I just had to paint, because I guess it was my way of trying to validate that wearing hats would be all right."

Inspired by the work of painting, Vicki surprised even herself and pledged several thousand dollars to the Susan G. Komen Breast Cancer Foundation to help fight breast cancer. The little white box of cards with their images of women wearing hats began selling by word of mouth, and sales quickly grew.

"I titled that series of paintings Sisterhood," Vicki explained, "because I do not have any family close to me at all. My family is a thousand miles away in Michigan. Even though I come from a large family, it was just too much to expect them to come. My husband worked long hours, and I felt this tremendous wave of 'I can't burden my husband, and I have kids at home.' My women friends were like family."

Tuesdays with Mary

One of my favorite paintings by Vicki is called "Tuesdays with Mary." It is a portrait of a charming little 80-something lady who inspired Vicki. Vicki told me Mary's story.

"For five years, I have had the pleasure of visiting Mary in a retirement facility. We became acquainted when I asked my church if there was volunteer work they needed me to do. They said, 'Well yes, a lady just called from out of state and is worried about her mother. She was wondering if someone would just go by and visit her.'

"Well, that someone became me, and Mary and I became good friends over the years. She uses a walker and has a permanent feeding tube in her stomach because of colon cancer. Mary reads a lot and stays sharp as a tack. She loves hearing about my boys, and I enjoy hearing of her life on the East Coast.

"Mary had so many different surgeries. You name it and Mary had it done. All that did not slow her down, and more importantly, she never complained. Several times I would take her for a ride in my little red convertible. We could not be gone too long, but Mary loved it. I told her I would be having breast surgery, and since I would be in the hospital, it might be a little while before I could come visit her again.

"Mary was the one who surprised me, because while I was in the hospital, Mary found a ride from the nursing facility, and on her walker, with her feeding tube, Mary came to visit me. Her visit was perhaps a simple gesture to some, but to me it was monumental. She could have had every possible excuse, yet she came to visit me."

A Little Help from My Friends

After her mastectomy, Vicki went home to recuperate and begin chemotherapy treatments. Yet before she started chemotherapy, a group of her friends surprised her and took her to the beach.

"I told them I did not think my doctor would let me go on such a trip, but they insisted I ask. I asked my surgeon, and to my surprise, off we went. Just the ride in the van to the beach was hilarious with this group of six women. Since I had just gotten out of surgery, I rested a lot, and they shopped. I rested, and they shopped some more...so I painted these women all sitting on the beach with me, and it all was so uplifting."

After a week at the beach, the girls returned home and Vicki started chemotherapy.

Vicki smiled when she told me about the friend who called and said, "I don't cook. I hate to cook, but I am going to pick up your things and take them to the cleaners."

Her gesture was just the kind of help Vicki welcomed most. "That was so honest and tremendously helpful in keeping a household going. I think we often underestimate simple gestures. We think it has to be something monumental to be memorable. Another friend decided she would make me some little pillows—several different sizes of these little pillows to prop myself up with, because after a mastectomy she thought I would need them. And I could not believe how often I used those little pillows. She was so talented in sewing, and that was such a memorable gift. We need not think, *My gift is not something monumental, I am too embarrassed to do anything.* Those little pillows were so wonderful when the time came to put them behind my neck or elbow."

Vicki was blessed by friends who brought food, especially during the summer when her boys were home. With a husband and three boys, mealtime could be demanding.

Another friend was instrumental in setting up an E-mail system. "She is a super organizer and set up my church friends, my artist friends, and my tennis friends, and they could log on and find out what day they could sign up to bring dinner."

To protect Vicki's privacy and allow her the needed rest, the family kept a cooler on the back porch. Friends would drop off dinner without having to disturb her on days when she could not get up to go to the door.

One night her youngest son was feeling sad, and when a neighbor brought over dinner, "his face just lit up," Vicki recalled, "because she came on into the kitchen to say hello. Usually friends dropped food off in the cooler, and he would not see anybody. The neighbor lady had her children with her, and as he greeted her, she gave him a big hug. I think that was all my son needed. We sat down to a home-cooked dinner that night, and he was able to get up from the table and go study. She brought a sense of normalcy back into our home. He really appreciated not only the dinner, but the hug as well."

Vicki emphasized how valuable it was for friends to bring food to her family. It was so important that she now wants to organize a Casserole Pantry at her church for those who might need some help like she did. "I know single mothers and the elderly will be the first ones we try to help," she said. "So many women do not have the kind of support that my church and my friends gave me. I always say, don't underestimate the power of a casserole, or an errand to the cleaners, and especially just a visit, like my friend Mary's."

Vicki said she also appreciated cards of encouragement. "One friend sent me a card every single day for six months. I learned what a value that was, to encourage with the gift of the written word. Some of the cards were funny, some were creative, and on some she would just write, 'Be strong, have courage.' Those cards meant so much to me that they inspired me to turn my artwork into stationery cards that can help lift others up."

Women Helping Women

The watercolor images that Vicki painted for her own therapy can now be used to encourage others. The power of women helping women had such a profound effect on Vicki that she made that initial, significant pledge to the Komen Breast Cancer Foundation, whose mission is to eradicate breast cancer as a life-threatening disease through the advancement of research, education, screening, and treatment.

As demand grew for the Sisterhood cards, Vicki often wondered about one lady in particular who frequently ordered several boxes of cards at once. What was she doing with all those boxes of stationery?

The mystery unraveled when Vicki found out the lady was a flight attendant for a major airline. She'd been sent one of the cards, read the story on the back, and ordered a set. She loved the cards and showed them to passengers on the airplane. Many of the passengers were purchasing boxes of them from the attendant.

Vicki and the flight attendant had never met; it was just the power of sisterhood once more. The flight attendant cherished the fact that the proceeds of the cards went to help find a cure for breast cancer, and she just wanted to help. Recently, Vicki and the flight attendant finally met for the first time. Both ladies were honored at a Komen Foundation luncheon for all the money they had raised together.

"That surely explains how I was getting orders from all over the country, and how we are getting the message out about sisterhood," Vicki laughed. "She is like my card-angel flying in the sky."

The flight attendant's efforts even led to a trip to Maine for Vicki. A lady who represented the Komen Foundation in the state of Maine had been given a card by a survivor who thought the card was wonderful. "They wondered if I would come be their guest artist during their big race event," Vicki said. "I designed a poster, and it was given as an award to their top volunteer. All this from someone sending a card. All this from sitting at home painting...pretty amazing."

Leading a Support Group

Now, once a month, Vicki and her friend Evelyn lead a breast cancer support group for about 25 women of all ages. Describing the members as single, married, young, and not so young, Vicki said they all have one thing in common, breast cancer. "We open each meeting with a prayer, and it becomes a time of sharing joys and concerns. It is a wonderful way to support and educate each other, as we all have different needs, questions, and fears. Fear of the unknown is omitted, because our group always has someone who has been through a similar problem."

Vicki pointed out how important it is for women with breast cancer to talk with other women who have also been through it. Some things nurses and doctors do not tell a patient, or even think to tell, simply because they have not been through it themselves, Vicki said. "A lot of the ladies in our group are on strong anticancer drugs, and can be reassured by someone else in the group who is also taking the drugs."

Women find comfort and support in one another as they deal with the varied effects of treatment. The journey is not the same for each person, but in a group, someone will know what to say. "Just like the fact of a woman losing her hair," Vicki explained. "When the three friends in the first hat party donned hats that day, we did not know who would lose their hair. As it turned out, Leslie and I did not lose our hair. However, Evelyn did. We all joked that our chemo-cocktail required different ingredients, and Evelyn's involved 'hair lose.'"

Through all the trials, the women still manage at times to find humor in their situations. "It seems to make us all feel better when we laugh," Vicki said. "Only one sweet face of our members has not been able to laugh yet, but she keeps coming back."

Lessons and Gifts

Other lessons and gifts have come via the humor she has shared in sisterhood. "Breast cancer has taught me to lighten up a bit," she said, "because I am not as serious about mishaps as I was before. I know there is plenty to be serious about, but it helps to laugh, too, and that is one thing this group does. It gives us back the gift of joy. That is a real gift in itself."

Admitting that help is needed, accepting help, and just saying thank you are other lessons that have come Vicki's way.

"Having breast cancer has taught me a lesson in how to receive, because that was always hard for me to do," Vicki said. "I was one of those women who would never ask for help, yet I was so blessed to have it pour in my door."

The journey of breast cancer can be a profound spiritual experience if we allow it to be. Learning how to receive the kindness of others and open our hearts is a powerful gift. "We all love that tough 'can do' attitude, but sometimes God brings us to our knees when we least expect it," Vicki said.

"I just turned 50 last week, and I have to be honest—I would love to have my body back. But I would not turn back the clock for anything. So much good has come out of this life experience. I feel I have changed for the better, and so has my husband. I feel so much more the love of my husband, and it is real obvious he loves me very, very much…and that means so much to me. Some husbands might run when there is trouble as serious as this. I was very blessed, because we are closer now and value each other more than ever. Some marriages will get better, and some will get worse. I was blessed; mine got better."

The Mission Field

Vicki's husband is a doctor, and a few years ago, she and their children went with him and other medical friends on a medical mission trip to Honduras. They stayed in touch with a friend from the mission field when they returned home. During her ordeal with breast cancer, Vicki received a letter from him that she regards as one of the most beautiful, meaningful letters of her life. The letter explained how this man devised a way for the circle of friends, all in different cities, to pray at 8 P.M. for Vicki and her family.

As Vicki described it, "I got a telephone call that evening from one family in particular that said they were celebrating their daughter's birthday, and they were in a family circle, holding hands praying for me along with all the other members of that mission trip. Prayer warriors were lifting my whole family up, and I received a flood of peace with God's plan for me as a wife, a mother, a friend, and an artist."

The prayers brought spiritual healing to Vicki's life, clearing the way for her to serve others. Applying her desire to serve God to the lessons she had learned in her battle with breast cancer, Vicki discovered, "My mission now is here at home. I was educated because of my friend Evelyn, who walked in front of me, and I give my name to any patient who has just begun to walk on this path. If I had not been given Evelyn's name, I don't know what I would have done. Evelyn and I both have decided that our missions don't have to be in faraway countries—they can be right at our own back door."

So much work begs to be done in the field of breast cancer. Women of all ages need education explaining how early detection can save a life. Most tumors, for example, are found through mammograms, not by self-detection, Vicki said. "I am working on painting more stationery note cards with the proceeds going to breast cancer research, because I have this need to give back. I have been blessed so much. And, too, I just want a cure for breast cancer!"

Vicki and her cards remind me about the story of three men building a cathedral. A passerby asks one man, who is digging a wall for the foundation, "What are you doing?" The man looks up in disbelief, and says with disgruntlement, "I am digging a hole."

The man kneeling next to a pile of stones is asked the same question. He looks up and answers the man, "Can't you see I am building a wall?"

Nearby, and whistling a cheerful tune, a third laborer pushes a cart full of dirt. Asked by the same man the very same question, the laborer, his face lit by joy, quickly replies, "I am building a cathedral!"

A box of cards may seem like just some pretty paper on which to pen notes, but Vicki sees in those cards a grand cathedral in sisterhood where, through the power of women helping women, there is no more breast cancer.

Breast cancer brings many lessons and gifts. It can teach you to lighten up, to embrace humor, to receive without going into overdrive. Breast cancer can initiate a profound spiritual experience, bringing clarity and guidance on how to live one's life.

*S*ometimes in life
we get washed up on shore, stranded out of
place, and find ourselves out of the swim of things.
Maybe we need the attention of others to help us back
into the teeming sea of life. Whatever our
particular situation, a positive attitude is
the best medicine ever.

CHAPTER NINE

The Best Medicine Ever

The mind, in addition to medicine, has powers to
turn the immune systems around.

JONAS SALK

DURING ONE OF MY MOST MEMORABLE VACATIONS, I spent a week with my family on Florida's Sanibel Captiva Island. I enjoyed sun, wind, and waves, but in particular, the beaches covered with seashells. The tides washed up a fresh display each night, and my sons and I spent hours each day collecting and admiring our newfound treasures from the sea.

We always lingered on the beach late in the day to watch the sun sink below the horizon. The boys and I still kept an eye out for that one perfect shell, even though we had grown tired of bending down and picking them up. My husband took pleasure just watching our efforts of collecting. But one evening, something caught his eye. He looked at me and silently pointed at this new treasure.

Samuel and I walked over to see what it was. A starfish shone back at us, washed up on shore. Gently picking it up, I inspected it more closely, noticing small movements from underneath. I tossed the starfish back into the waves, as if sending it back home.

Samuel looked at me and asked, "Will it live, Mama?"

"I think it will, and we will give it every chance," I softly replied.

Samuel and I stood staring out toward the sea, hoping in our hearts that the starfish's life would be renewed.

I remember that starfish now every time I hear about a new breast cancer patient. Washed up on shore, at least for the moment, stranded out of place, the object of someone's concern. Will she live? "We will give her every chance," I want to answer.

With a breast cancer diagnosis, we might feel for a time that we're out of the swim of things, away from life. But then someone picks us up—the doctor, our husband, a friend, a relative, ourselves, God—and then we are back in the teeming sea of life. And somehow, through it all, we have been renewed.

Though my friend Dian Gregory now lives in the U.S., she grew up in a place as beautiful and inspirational as the island I visited in Florida. Her beaches of home were on the small island of Bequia, north off the coast of Trinidad, in the West Indies. One of the most positive personalities I know, Dian is always smiling and laughing. I wonder if her beautiful spirit has something to do with being raised in the island's air.

I love being around Dian. When I went to visit her on the first of December, a wreath hung on her door, a Christmas tree twinkled in the window, and she met me with her usual big smile, welcoming me into her home with a hug. The wind blew cold as she closed the door. Dian's natural warmth dispelled the cold as she turned away from the wintry air and invitingly offered, "Come on back."

I followed behind her to the back of her luxurious suburban home and into a sunroom, where we looked out over a perfectly manicured garden and clear blue swimming pool. We took our seats on a plump, comfortable sofa. As Dian curled her feet beneath her, I noticed she was barefooted. She caught me looking and laughed, "I still have my island feet!" This was in Texas, so even in December the ground was not frozen. But it was still cold! The swimming pool outside the door sparkled and glistened in the Texas sun and even looked inviting on such a cold day. Dian, who left her islands over 40 years ago, had still managed to keep her tropical heart.

"Let me show you a picture," she offered, in her beautiful, crisp English accent. Displaying a large aerial photograph of the tropical island where she grew up, she pointed out significant features.

"See the coconut groves, and here are the orange groves on the island." Pointing to a clearing, she said, "That is where our home on the plantation was. The island over there is St. Vincent. It is 12 miles away, and those reefs that are about half a mile out are where my brother and I used to swim out to snorkel."

What looked to me like paradise and the perfect life was not so to Dian, however. "Mother and Father were very strict," she told me. "The English headmaster came to our home for private tutoring, so we did not get to go to a traditional school. Once I wanted my hair cut, because it was so long I could sit on it, but my father wouldn't see to it. They were very, very strict on my two brothers and me. My father did a lot of work politically in the islands."

Dian told me that the Queen of England had awarded her father the title Member of the British Empire. She rose from the sofa and invited me to come have a look at a small, satin-lined case. Situated in a place of honor, the lighted display case held her father's medal, along with a certificate that actually bore the Queen's signature. Dian also told me the story of Winston Churchill's visit to Bequia and her father's meeting with him. Dian's mother and father have since passed on, and so Dian holds in safekeeping the assortment of family treasures.

As soon as she turned 20, Dian left the islands, spending every penny she had on travel. Her travels led to her meeting and marrying her husband, but marriage didn't slow her down. "When Dave and I first got married, my mother had an address book just for me, because we kept moving around so much," Dian said. "We traveled all over and would just pick up and go. A couple of years after we were married we visited a tiny little seaside fishing village in Devon, England, and we decided that would be a lovely place to live for a while. It was just gorgeous, picture perfect, and it captured our hearts. There our son Andy was born."

A remote, rural location, Devon had only a country doctor to deliver a baby in breech position. Andy was born mentally challenged, but at 37, he's doing great.

With her typical big smile, Dian told me that Andy lives in a home not too far from hers, with four others. He has a job, never misses a day of work, and "is so happy and upbeat," she said. I smiled back at her, because her description of Andy's personality certainly reminded me of his mother!

Dian's Battle with Breast Cancer

Like the other women I interviewed, Dian is a survivor of breast cancer. I knew that over the years she had been a volunteer in the effort to educate women about breast cancer. When I asked her how she became involved, her answer was simple—"a mammogram."

Nine years ago, a yearly mammogram had detected a calcification. "I learned that it was malignant," she said, "and was given the choice of a lumpectomy or mastectomy by my doctor. My own instinct was to have the mastectomy, but I did not know anybody who had breast cancer to talk about this with.

"My husband called our friend Peter who was an orthopedic surgeon in Canada, and said, 'Peter, we just do not know what to do.' Dave explained what was going on. Peter recommended what my gut feeling was, and that settled it for me. Someone I trusted helped make the decision."

Dian elected to have a mastectomy with reconstruction. Today, because there are so many new treatments and "everything has just gotten better and better," she isn't sure that she would choose the same way as nine years ago.

But for women who do choose, like her, to have a mastectomy with reconstruction, Dian recommends having both surgeries at once. "When I came out, I had a breast, just like when I went in. To go back six months later to rebuild would be tough. I was just ready to move on, and the miracle of the surgery is that I did not feel disfigured."

After the surgery was over, Dian quickly recovered and felt fine. The hardest part for her was making the decision to take the chemotherapy treatment that her doctor recommended. She did not want to go through with it.

She went to another doctor for a second opinion. He told her, "You have had your breast removed, and you have gone through hours of reconstruction. You have done all of that, and you are not going to take the final step, and do something to try and eradicate it from your system?"

Dian agreed to the chemotherapy. "I just needed for him to come out and say it. I never looked back from then on."

Dian's husband went to every treatment with her and was there for everything. He even took a notepad to take notes on what the doctors were saying. "It was another set of ears to hear," Dian reported, "because I was sort of numb and don't remember everything."

While Dian felt blessed by her husband's support, many women are not so fortunate. "I have learned through my volunteer work that if the husband is not supportive in the very beginning, it is tough on a marriage," Dian said. "If the husband refuses to accept what has happened, the marriage usually goes on the rocks."

Dian found chemotherapy tough, just as she had expected. For her, the surgery was easier than the chemo. But she kept a positive attitude, knowing that with every treatment she was getting better. "I would tell myself to be positive. I did not have a why-me? attitude, because breast cancer happens and it happened to me. I did not do this to myself. It just happened."

Dian decided she would do everything she could to get it out of her system. "I did get nauseated from the chemo, but I got some tablets that really helped. If I smelled bacon cooking it would make me sick. My husband says I can smell something a mile away. And I guess I was really tired too, but I never stopped."

After one chemotherapy treatment, Dian and her husband drove to Florida for a week. "Talk about therapy...watching the ocean was wonderful," she remembered.

"I was not going to let this stop my life. Life goes on, and I don't think I should just stop living. In this day and age, a person diagnosed should never have a negative attitude, because there is so much helpful technology out there."

Dian asked her doctors lots of questions, writing them down first so she wouldn't forget to ask them all. "I learned not to take everything at face value that the doctors said. That is why I had to question everything—I wanted to know why. The doctors could not possibly know all the questions I would have; they could not read my mind." Asking questions helped eliminate the fear factor and brought Dian peace of mind. "When I understood what all was going on, it took away the fear," she said.

Dealing with Hair Loss

While taking a shower on the fourteenth day of chemotherapy, Dian lost all her hair. As she watched it go down the drain, she felt hurt. The hurt didn't come from a sense of pride, she said. "I don't have words to explain how it felt. It was such a sinking feeling."

Dian tried on a wig, hated it, and chose not to wear one at all. Although most people did not say anything about her appearance when she was out, Dian appreciated those who did. Time and again, the women I interviewed said they preferred people to interact with them rather than ignore them. Not every woman is the same, and sensitivity is required, but generally, the women I talked with welcomed the concern of strangers. Dian made an important point when she noted, "It was all right to say something."

She did not want anyone to feel sad about her situation; she simply appreciated the fact that they cared. "Sometimes a child would point and tell their mother to look. As their mother frantically tried to quiet their discovery, I would go over and tell the mother, 'It is all right, just tell them I have had a medical treatment that caused me to lose my hair.' The truth always seemed to work wonders. Now I really make it a point to say something to someone who might be going through chemotherapy, because I know what it is like to be there."

Sometimes people were insensitive in their comments, however. "One of the ladies in my canasta card group told me not to worry about my hair, that was just pride," Dian said. "It really hurt my feelings."

But two years after Dian was diagnosed, that canasta friend called Dian to offer an apology. "I really did not know what she was talking about," Dian said. "I had forgotten." But the woman explained that she herself was now going through breast cancer treatment, and she realized in losing her own hair how hurtful her comment on Dian's pride, said years ago, must have been.

Family and Friends

Dian is close to her daughter and son-in-law, who live within five miles of her home. She also had great support from her husband.

"My extended family," she explained, "is our circle of friends. I am 62 years old and have always lived away from family since I was 20, when I moved away from our tiny island to see the rest of the world."

Even her closest friends had a hard time talking to her about her breast cancer, she said. "I would try to set them at ease and just tell them, 'I know you don't know what to say, but I am feeling great.' Since my friends were so uncomfortable talking about it, I would get it out in the open…. I know they wanted to say something, but probably did not know what to say. Anything in a positive direction would have been wonderful, because I was always trying to keep my attitude in the right direction. I look back now—it was a hard year, but it was so worth it."

Because she had so many friends, Dian never felt the need to go to a support group. "I guess I am sort of hardheaded and just knew I was not going to let this get me down. I wanted to wade through it, do it, get rid of it, and get on with my life. I was so blessed with friends that I did not want to go to a support group and run the risk of hearing negativity. I had a lot of treasured friends, and they did not always understand what I was going through, but they were always there for me. I think I kind of had my own private little support group."

A Positive Attitude

Dian did everything she could possibly do to get well. She chooses not to dwell on her cancer, and often goes days at a time without thinking about it. "It does not consume my life," she said. "When I am standing in the shower drying off, I don't even see my scar anymore. Life after breast cancer is wonderful, because I have learned so much."

Going through diagnosis, surgery, and treatment gave her a stronger faith, she said, because she knew she could get through it. A lot of good things came out of her experience. "I guess that is why I have no patience with doom and gloom. I just do not like to hear anything negative about any part of this."

Dian raised her voice. "If I cut my foot, and it heals, I don't go around thinking about it. So why should I treat this any differently?"

One of the positive ways in which Dian has dealt with her cancer is by giving back to other women what she has learned. She goes to regular meetings at the Komen Breast Cancer Foundation, which disseminates all the new information that comes out about breast cancer. "I work in the education department of the foundation where we go and set up a table at a mall or corporate center—anywhere there will be lots of women. There we hand out brochures, answer questions, and offer all sorts of information."

Women often pass by without stopping to look or ask questions. But as Dian said, "We have come a long way in nine years. I've seen a big difference. People's attitudes have changed. They are not as afraid of breast cancer anymore. More and more women are educated to the fact that having a mammogram can save a life, and that early detection is still the key to saving a life."

Once, when working at a department store with a display of educational brochures, Dian noticed women glancing at the information, and then looking the other way. Now, she said, more and more young girls are listening and paying attention. "Breast cancer seems to be hitting younger and younger women," she said. "There seems to be no age barrier or color barrier."

Dian goes back once a year for checkups, but otherwise her life is pretty much back to normal. This year will be her last year to check in with her oncologist, she said. "They like to track their patients for ten years. Then I just go back to my regular doctor after that."

With her ever-present smile, Dian affirmed: "I know that breast cancer is life threatening, but one must keep a positive attitude." Dian encouraged women not to wear their condition on their faces, because there is so much that can be done.

The lesson I learned from Dian is that a positive attitude cannot be in a pill, it has to be in our hearts. Doctors cannot prescribe it, because we can only give it to ourselves.

When asked for some special words of wisdom, Mother Teresa of Calcutta replied, "Smile at those you live with."

And Plato told us, "The face is the mirror of the soul."

Another writer put it this way, "Each of us is a living advertisement of how we think and feel."

Dian's 62 years of living prove that no matter what the diagnosis, a positive attitude is the best medicine ever.

For as he thinketh in his heart, so is he…
PROVERBS 23:7 (KJV)

⌒

Do not take at face value everything your doctors tell you. They cannot read your mind and therefore cannot possibly know all of your questions. Asking questions brings peace of mind and helps eliminate the fear factor.

⌒

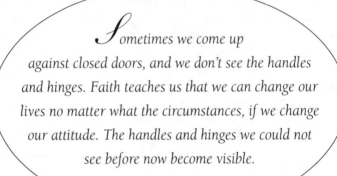

*S*ometimes we come up against closed doors, and we don't see the handles and hinges. Faith teaches us that we can change our lives no matter what the circumstances, if we change our attitude. The handles and hinges we could not see before now become visible.

CHAPTER TEN

The Only Way to Win

God takes our pieces and gives us peace.
ANONYMOUS

WHEN I STARTED MY SOAP COMPANY, Alda's Forever, 11 years ago, Bill Morris offered to help. His wife was my oldest son's art teacher, and we became acquainted from school. Bill had retired from his career in the world of computers, which included a time at the Kennedy Space Center working with rockets and spaceships. Now he was enjoying being a grandfather to his own children, and to a classroom of first graders, too. From providing classroom assistance to helping make stage scenery for the class play, Mr. Bill was always there.

Bill stopped by to visit me one day because he'd found out I was in a panic and needed help in organizing my incoming orders. I was working in our new barn with Bill's wife and several other friends who had pitched in to help. We were making the soap, packaging it, and shipping it out all over the country. With both hands I handed Bill a shoebox stuffed with papers. I also wore a "what am I going to do" look on my face. Toward the end of the week, Bill handed me an organized computer printout telling exactly how much soap I needed to make to fill my orders.

With the leadership of my husband, the business I started in our barn has now grown into a 12-acre complex that includes a wholesale manufacturing and distribution warehouse in the industrial area of our city. Bill believed in our efforts, watched us grow, and stood faithfully by our side every step of the way. He continues to work behind the scenes within our operation, helping to keep mainframes, networking, software, and hardware all running smoothly.

Bill always seems to slip in, get the job done, and slip out again. Perhaps because of the way in which he goes about his work, many of us never knew about his daughter's illness. Just recently, my husband mentioned to Bill that I was working on a book about breast cancer. Bill never looked up from his computer screen, yet he crossed his arms and placed them in his lap. In his quiet manner of speaking, he replied after some thought, "My daughter had that four years ago."

When my husband told me what Bill had said, he began the conversation with "You are not going to believe this," and he was right. Mouth agape, I could not imagine that I did not know about Bill's daughter, Kathy. My husband and I stuttered almost in unison, "Why did we not know about that?" Kathy lived just two houses down the street from Bill. Together we had rejoiced in his granddaughter's wedding and the birth of her two children, yet somehow I did not know that Bill's daughter had been diagnosed with breast cancer.

I called Kathy and during our first visit found out why I had not known this earlier. Very strong and stoic, Kathy dealt with her cancer in her own way. She told no one outside her immediate family and only one person at her work.

During the course of interviews and discussions with many women, I learned that each person handles breast cancer in her own way, defining her path individually. Kathy was very private about her experience. Her faith never wavered as she went about her business of daily living.

Kathy's Story

Alone in a hotel room while on an out-of-town assignment, Kathy rolled over one morning before getting dressed for work and felt a lump in her breast. "I knew immediately what it was, even though I had never felt it before," she told me. "I came home and went right to the doctor, knowing that I was late for my mammogram and now there was a lump. In the past I had been so good to go once a year for a mammogram, but I had been so busy lately that time had slipped by me—and now it had been two years."

Although the news did not devastate her, Kathy knew it was not good. The realization took a while to sink in, she said. "I could not believe that it was happening to me. I was like everybody else and thought that it always happens to someone else…not me."

Once she accepted the situation, she took off work for two weeks and had a lumpectomy. Some of her lymph nodes were also removed. The lump was malignant, which meant additional treatments. Kathy set up a schedule of chemotherapy and radiation treatments and went right back to work.

Kathy's husband of 26 years was very supportive. He went with her to the first two appointments, but after that, she did not want anybody to take her to her appointments or come pick her up—she just wanted to do it herself.

Her mom was upset because Kathy wanted to go through chemotherapy alone, but Kathy found the treatment to be easy. "All I did was sit in a big chair with an IV in my arm and watch TV," she said. "The chemo did make me really tired, but I would lie down and rest for a bit. If I had to work out of town, I would just lie down and take a nap before I had to get up and go."

Looking to the Future

The only thing that really bothered her, Kathy said, was losing her hair. "I would go in the bathroom and brush my hair and it would just fall out by the handfuls. It was like I was brushing my hair *off* my head."

Kathy was very practical and matter-of-fact in the way that she dealt with her hair loss. Looking to the future, she started wearing a wig *before* she lost her hair. People got used to seeing her in a wig, and no one ever said anything. "I guess they just thought I was having a bad hair day," Kathy commented.

Kathy bought a pageboy-style wig with a headband, which made the wig easy to keep on even when her hair was all gone. "But it sure did itch!" she said. "When I would get home, the wig would come off, and I would wear a soft cap or a hat."

Kathy was able to manage her schedule around her treatments and never missed a day of work. "I worked through it all, and I don't think that anybody even noticed. In my job, I travel to small towns in Arkansas, Tennessee, Missouri, and Mississippi, and I am away from home for most of the week," she said. A field technician for a grocery store chain, Kathy helped train checkout clerks on the cash registers and scanners in each store that she visited.

"I did not make a big deal out of all this, and I did not tell too many people," Kathy said. "I never questioned it, but just accepted it for what it was. The main thing that I knew from being a Christian was that everything would turn out okay. I had been raised in the church, and through my upbringing, I knew that I was always going to be able to handle whatever was handed to me. I was praying, my husband was praying, my mom and dad were praying for me, and my church was praying for me. That was all the help I needed."

Kathy tried to stay upbeat and positive throughout her treatments. When any negative or bad thoughts would start to creep in, she would find something to keep her busy. "I knew every day was one more day of this behind me," she said.

Staying Busy

I was amazed at Kathy's determination not to let any of this slow her down, especially when she told me she'd driven for four hours to pick up her toddler granddaughter. Kathy's daughter is in the Navy and had just had a new baby, so Kathy thought it would make it easier on her daughter to have only one baby to take care of instead of two. "With everybody doing a little bit, it was not hard on anybody," Kathy said, "and especially since my mom and dad lived down the road."

Kathy believes that the secret to her life going so well the last four years is her desire and determination to stay busy. "I did not want to dwell on it, nor did I want anybody else to dwell on it either. I knew in my heart that I was going to get better, and I knew what I had to do to get better. Staying busy and plowing right on through my job and helping to take care of my granddaughter was my therapy. I believed that the best medicine ever was to stay busy and get on with living."

Sometimes the chemotherapy made Kathy nauseated, but she got over that, too. She tried one of the antinausea drugs but did not like it, so she decided to go without it. "I would have to stop and eat something, but again that is why my job was fantastic," she said. "The company I worked for was very supportive of the schedule that I worked. They let me do what I needed to do for them at my own pace, and I continued doing what I needed to do for them.

"I really did not have any problems at all. My doctors were so wonderful, and I trusted what they told me I should do. My oncologist would take the time to answer my questions, and I understood what my treatment plan was thoroughly."

A Right Time for Everything

Kathy shared a Bible verse with me from the book of Ecclesiastes that inspired and comforted her during her encounter with breast cancer. "I just thought that this was my time, and there would be a time to heal," she said.

> *There is a right time for everything: a time to be born, a time to die; a time to plant; a time to harvest…a time to destroy; a time to rebuild.*
> ECCLESIASTES 3:1-3 (TLB)

Since her own diagnosis, Kathy has known several people she works with and several friends who have also been diagnosed with breast cancer. "I was really touched when I found out that *I* was the first person they called. One by one, they would call and want to find out what all this was going to be like," she told me. "It was personally rewarding that I could be their support, answer their questions, and calm their fears."

Some of her friends were very fearful, but to counter that, Kathy told them they had to take the reins and go with it, because breast cancer happens. Her practical, straightforward approach included the advice: "We do not know what caused it, we could not prevent it, and we just have to get rid of it. You have to be strong, face it, and get over it."

Kathy believes it helped those she talked with to hear from a personal standpoint stories about losing hair and some of the side effects of chemotherapy, such as nausea. Now there are more effective medicines for helping counter nausea. Two of her friends who had mastectomies talk with her at work or at home about their situations, and Kathy said it helps them all "to do a little venting."

Kathy is a marvelous example of women who find and make their own support groups. Although she never formally attended a support group, because, she said, "I did not need to go talk about it," nonetheless, she serves as a listening post and helper to other women who find themselves facing breast cancer. Essentially, she heads her own private support group.

Kathy is still taking the drug tamoxifen. She goes every six months to have a bone scan and a mammogram. Told that she would have to take tamoxifen for five years, she is now in her fourth year. After that, her six-month checkups will extend to a yearly checkup. Her doctor recommended some preventive medicines, too, to keep recurrence down in the future.

Kathy is the perfect poster model for optimism. With all the doors that she came up against, she saw that they had handles and hinges. The pessimist would have seen a closed door as having locks and latches.

Kathy's determination and courage come from the roots of her upbringing and her daily walk with God. Using Kathy's example, we can change our lives no matter what the circumstances—if we change our attitude.

When I asked Kathy if breast cancer was the worst thing that had ever happened to her, she quietly said no. With a hushed voice, she told of losing her infant son only hours after birth. "I knew that if I could make it through the days after coming home from the hospital and not getting to bring my baby home, I could walk through anything that could happen to me," she said.

Like many of the other women with whom I talked, Kathy emphasized one of the big lessons she learned from her experience: "Go get a mammogram! It is one of the best things that any woman can do for herself. Don't put it off because of fear of the results. Finding cancer early is still the best weapon for beating it."

Christian Faith

Since talking with Kathy, I believe I have found the reason that her father never told me about her breast cancer. Bill did not mention it to anybody because Kathy kept right on going. Her Christian faith and her strong-willed spirit kept her on her daily walk. I opened my Bible and read the scripture verse, Ecclesiastes 3:1-3, which meant so much to her. It continues on:

> *Everything is appropriate in its own time. But though God has planted eternity in the hearts of men, even so, many cannot see the whole scope of God's work from beginning to end.*
>
> Ecclesiastes 3:11 (TLB)

Bill still drifts in and out of our office when we need help with our computer systems. My husband and I were thrilled to receive an invitation to a fiftieth wedding anniversary celebration for Bill and Marie. Kathy and her family will be right there along with the rest of Bill's family and friends. Kathy knows that with God's help, she will win her battle with breast cancer. Not only is she winning, she sees her walk with God as the only way.

Maintain your faith, and go about the business of daily living. Be strong, face it, then take the reins and go with it, because breast cancer happens. Know that God is in charge, God has a purpose for everything, and your attitude will make all the difference in the world as to the quality of your daily life.

The Only Way to Win

It takes a bit of courage
And a little self-control,
And some grim determination,
If you want to reach your goal.
It takes a deal of striving
And a firm and stern-set chin,
No matter what the battle,
If you really want to win.

There is no easy path to glory,
There's no rosy road to fame.
Life, however we may view it,
Is no simple parlor game;
But its prizes call for fighting,
For endurance and for grit;
For a rugged disposition
And a don't-know-when-to-quit.

You must take a blow or give one,
You must risk and you must lose,
And expect that in the struggle,
You will suffer from the bruise,
But you must not wince or falter,
If a fight you once begin;
Be strong and face the battle—
For that's the only way to win.

AUTHOR UNKNOWN

When
an era of our life reaches an end, we need to
let go and make a heartfelt transition into the new.
Life changes us and presents us with choices. God is ever-
present in the gift of each new day.

CHAPTER ELEVEN

Pink Ribbon Pin

One cannot get through life without pain....What we can do is choose how to use the pain life presents to us.

BERNIE SIEGEL, M.D.

THE OLDER I GET, THE MORE I AM SURE OF change. Life is a journey, and we keep moving on, sometimes encountering forks in the road where we must make a choice, sometimes encountering boulders and other obstacles, where we must make another sort of choice. Most of the time we can never go back along this road—not that we would want to. But when we think about going back and changing something, we travel a path of memory that leads us into recognizing either something good that can come out of change, or something that we cannot accept. And sometimes when we travel this path of memory, it leaves us empty.

Studebaker cars, steam engines, and Elvis will never be brought back again. Each changed our life in some way, each had its strengths and weaknesses, but time remembers only the good. We find ourselves wanting to hold on. Instead, we need to let go.

It is my hope that, when we realize an era has come to an end, we will be able to make a heartfelt transition into the new.

How we perceive any event in our life and the attitude we bring to it can either hold us up or move us on. Although it is hard to see the good that can come from something so terrible as breast cancer, the way in which we move through it can greatly ennoble us if we let it.

Debbie's Story

Debbie Schatz was 39 and turning 40. Like the rest of us, Debbie was told by her doctor that upon turning 40, it is a good idea to get a baseline mammogram for future reference in preventing breast cancer. Debbie got her baseline mammogram, and two weeks later she received a letter in the mail saying that a lump had been detected on her X-rays.

"A letter!" Debbie told me. "I was so shocked, because I had sort of even forgotten that I had the mammogram and dismissed it. I thought I had done what I needed to do and that was that. When I got my letter, all I could think about was the old movie *Letter to Three Wives*. It was the movie about three women's letters that got lost in the mail and how their lives were different because they never received their letter."

As Debbie described it, when she received the letter, she "went crazy." She made an appointment for another mammogram, and a biopsy proved the lump to be malignant. She had surgery and radiation treatments, which she found to be very scary. That was 15 years ago.

Debbie could think of only one distant cousin in California who'd had breast cancer. Otherwise, she knew no one who had been diagnosed with it. "I was just so taken aback, floored, because no one else in my family had breast cancer," she said. "It certainly did not run in my family. I can just remember thinking, this cannot be happening to me!"

Although publicly breast cancer was a hush-hush topic at that time, people nonetheless came rising up from everywhere to be supportive of her and what she was going through. Among her circle of friends, Debbie was the first to have an experience with cancer.

"We were all in our thirties, and I had one or two friends whose parents had cancer, but I was the first in my age group of the people that I knew to go through this," she said. "And sad to say, I have certainly not been the last."

Confronting Emotions

Debbie struggled with her emotions. "I was just so fearful. The first couple of months, I used to cry at night. I did not know about cancer, and to me cancer was cancer. I did not know about the different stages, and I did not have anybody to ask. I got to the point where I decided I was going to fight this with everything that I had. I was not ready to give up, although I did not know if I would ever get well. I think it probably took me a year to convince myself that I would be okay."

Because Debbie's lymph nodes were not involved, her doctors did not recommend chemotherapy. "Now, even if women do not have nodes involved, chemotherapy is recommended as a preventive measure," she said. "I just had radiation, and again, I never knew anyone who had gone through radiation treatments. I was told nothing about side effects, which were not that bad, although I was sore and red. But the worst part was not knowing what to expect."

Debbie went to radiation treatments five times a week for six weeks and was "absolutely exhausted" from the treatments. The schedule in and of itself made her tired, she said. She tried not to complain, because radiation had been her choice based on what the doctors had offered her.

"I kept my breast and opted for a lumpectomy," she said. "If I had chosen a mastectomy, I would not have had the radiation, but I was given that choice."

Despite being upset, Debbie felt clear about what was happening. "I went with my gut feeling and had the lumpectomy, but I told myself that if I woke up and wanted to have the mastectomy, I would just go right back and have the surgery. I was determined not to live my life in fear, so I would pray about doing the right thing."

Like a lot of other women going through similar situations, Debbie felt stressed; so her doctor put her on antidepressants. "I really had trouble snapping out of it, but I knew I would eventually with the passing of time."

Debbie's doctor told her about a support group that had started recently. She went to the group for a while, but it was composed mostly of older women. Their issues and concerns were not the same as hers. Her biggest concern was whether or not she could get pregnant and have a healthy baby.

"This was a big issue for me, because I was still young and not married," Debbie said. "I was searching for answers, because it seemed that nobody had done a study about radiation. One doctor I talked to just looked at me funny and wanted to know if I wanted my child to become an orphan! Again I was devastated. Finally I asked my radiologist, telling him I was not married and not ready to have a baby, but wanted to know the possibilities. He was very kind about it, but thought it would be better if I adopted a baby."

In looking back, Debbie said that she does not regret having breast cancer, but she does regret never having a child. The answers she got from her doctors made her unsure and sad, because she was not ready to give up that dream.

Life Itself Is a Blessing

"I know that there are worse things than having cancer," Debbie told me. "But that has just been my personal worst. Yet so many wonderful things came out of it that I would not change it at all. I only had one sister, and I am the 'big' sister. We were not always so close, and the best thing to come out of all this was our relationship."

Debbie and her sister now talk several times a day. "I think it has only been four today," Debbie said, laughing. "We are so close now, and I adore my niece. It made me realize what is

really important in the larger scheme of things—my relationship with God, and my relationships with my family. I do not
think that I was ever a real 'poor little ole me' person, but I
know that I am not now. It takes a lot to rock my boat now.
There are just worse things to get upset over."

Blessed by tons of support from her family, Debbie never
went anywhere alone. Family, friends, and other people were
there to show her that they cared. "When I was in the hospital,
I had 35 different people send me flowers. This was just so
bizarre to me and really woke me up, because some of those
people I had not spoken to in ages."

Debbie's experience with breast cancer made her "very, very
spiritual," she said. "I pray every single night now, and I don't
think I ever did that in my life."

Many women I spoke with found themselves closer to God
during their battle with breast cancer. They relied on faith,
Scripture, and prayer to see them through. For Debbie, breast
cancer fully awakened her to God's presence.

"I am so thankful now and grateful just to be alive," she
said. "Before I don't think I ever even thought about it. I guess
I just took it for granted. But now, I realize that life itself is a
blessing, and I am grateful for God's gift to me of each day. Each
day now is a great thing, full of opportunities for me to do
something for my family and others."

The lessons of breast cancer do not come easy. In Debbie's
life, it took a while for everything to make sense. "I finally got to
that point and realized all the wonderful things that have happened, and all the things that I am thankful for," she said.
Debbie decided that instead of making her own life miserable
because of what happened, she would rather make her life
better. She noticed, in fact, that her life had already gotten better.

Starting a New Business

"Slowly I started healing and getting back into the swing of
life, but it was very hard for me because I was not sure what to

do," she said. "I started volunteering at an AIDS charity event because I felt like giving back would be helpful, not only to others, but to me, too."

At the charity event, someone invited Debbie to a breakfast where a group was trying to start a chapter of the Komen Breast Cancer Foundation. The group members were making plans for the first Race for the Cure in New York. "It was a time when I was ready to really sink my teeth into doing something," Debbie said. She started working for the Komen Foundation and served on their executive board of directors for nine years. It was a volunteer position that Debbie found purposeful in creating breast cancer awareness.

Because of her work with the foundation, Debbie was asked to speak at women's groups and business luncheons all over the city. At one particular luncheon she decided that she wanted to wear a pin to signify the cause. Living only two blocks from Bloomingdale's department store, Debbie searched there and all over the city but could not find a pin to represent breast cancer awareness. The seed of a new business had been planted in Debbie's fertile imagination.

Debbie visited a jeweler friend and asked if he could make a pin to match her pencil drawing and then enamel it in pink. She ordered six of the pink ribbon designs.

"I was working in the publishing business at the time and took time off to speak at the luncheon. One of the people who happened to be at that luncheon was John, the editor-in-chief of *Good Housekeeping* magazine. He and I were on the same board at the Race for the Cure. He came up to me after the luncheon, and I gave him one of my six pins. He thanked me and told me if there was ever anything that he could do to help, to let him know.

"I asked John that day to put the pin in his magazine, with the intent that we would donate a portion of any profits to the Komen Foundation. He asked me if I had a post office box number, and I had to tell him I did not, but by the next morning I would have one.

"The very next day I got up early and walked across the street to my post office and got the box. I called John's secretary, told her I had the box, and gave her the number. Looking back, I don't know if John really expected me to follow up that quickly, but I did, and he ended up putting a tiny two-inch ad in his magazine. The ad was placed in the magazine on a page where I thought no one would even see it, much less respond to it. I called it my 'Pin to Win,' which a reader could order by sending in a check to my new post office box. To my surprise, I had over a thousand orders, and that started my business."

Each year since designing the pin, Debbie has tried to come up with one new product, for which she donates a portion of the proceeds to breast cancer awareness. Her latest is pink nail polish. She gave it the tag line "help nail breast cancer," a reminder, she said, "to look at your nails and do a self-exam."

Women need to remember to take care of their bodies, and no one is going to do it for them. The nail polish, she said, "has literally reached around the world, because I just sent nail polish to Sweden! I wanted to create things that were attractive yet in some fashion were an awareness factor for all women…a little reminder."

Debbie has a 23-year-old niece who continues to serve as a reminder to Debbie of what she's fighting for. She does not want breast cancer to be part of her niece's life. "I felt that if we could make women aware at an earlier age, that would be a good thing," Debbie said.

"Now this little pin and the business it created has become the basis of my living. It lets me be my own boss, and even though it is a small company, I am doing what I love."

Debbie believes that she has made a difference through her business. Women have sent her some amazing letters telling her what this pin means and how it has touched people's lives. "It feels so good to have been a part of something that is fulfilling a purpose, because part of the money goes back into cancer groups every year," Debbie said.

"This year I am especially pleased to be working with the Young Survivor Coalition, because they deal with cancer in women under the age of 40. I was one of those women, and there was nowhere for me to go. They have questions and needs that are unique to their age group—I know because I have been there and had those questions, and the answers were hard to find. So just the fact that there is now a group like this, and that I can help, is really exciting to me."

Debbie has designed special pink ribbon pins for several groups. "I have done pins with a sneaker on the pink ribbon for a running club. I have done a pin with a motorcycle on the pink ribbon for a motorcycle group. I have done pins of faith, with a cross on the pink ribbon and a Star of David on the pink ribbon."

She also designed an African American pink ribbon pin, one that she found particularly significant because statistics show that this group of women has a higher mortality rate from breast cancer. The reason is *not* that it has a higher occurrence rate, Debbie reported, but that breast cancer is detected too late, or not at all. Awareness plays an important role in survival.

Debbie could not bring herself to create a pink ribbon pin with the American flag on it, she said, perhaps because it hit too close to home after the tragedy of September 11. She was on the phone that day with her accountant, whose office was in the second of the World Trade Center towers. He was killed in the tragedy. One day, however, Debbie got a call from a Boy Scout in Pennsylvania whose mother had breast cancer, and he wanted to wear a pin on his uniform for her. "That phone call convinced me that there was a need, and I could fill it," she said.

Breast Center

Besides serving on the board for the Komen Foundation, Debbie finds time to volunteer at the Memorial Sloan-Kettering

Cancer Center, which treats more breast-cancer patients than any other cancer center in the nation. Located right in her neighborhood, the hospital has a Breast Center where Debbie volunteers every Tuesday, something she has done since it opened nine years ago. She talks with patients and their families, brings them coffee, and tries to ease their fears. She reassures, comforts, and encourages them.

"They do not want to be where they are, and I know how that feels," Debbie said. "I go visit with the patients before and after they are diagnosed and tell them that I have been in their shoes. They look at me with concern in their eyes because this is the last place they would like to be."

Sloan-Kettering's Breast Center features special chemotherapy rooms that Debbie described as "gorgeous." Each little private room has a television and a sliding glass door that looks out onto the atrium.

"Although it is not a luxurious spa, I try to make the patients' time there less stressful by reassuring them," Debbie said. "The patients in this room have already had their surgery, and they have already been through a lot. They are doing their follow-up treatment, and it is easier to talk with them... because they know they have cancer, and they know what stage of treatment they're in. Since most people are on a weekly schedule, they usually come in on the same day of the week. My Tuesday patients are usually people that I get to see more than once."

Debbie learned through volunteer work that she, like everybody, has strengths and weaknesses and that there are some volunteer jobs she is not comfortable doing. She especially loves to volunteer on holidays, and has found her niche, she said, in giving comfort through encouraging words.

"I give them encouragement, too, by letting them see I made it through all of this just fine, and they can, too, especially when I know that someone is on her last treatment. It's always such a joyous occasion," she said.

"Plenty of days, I have been shocked at the thought of what I do. I am so thankful that this volunteer program found me, and that I found it. So many people I know will never forget me, and I will never forget them...even though we will probably never see each other again. Through all this, I think that I have found the secret to a happy life...I have found a way to make the tragedy of breast cancer work in a meaningful and purposeful way."

Searching for Meaning

> *Diseases can be our spiritual flat tires—disruptions in our lives that seem to be disasters at the time but end by redirecting our lives in a meaningful way.*
>
> BERNIE SIEGEL, M.D.

Debbie went through several years of searching for a meaning to all of this. "Then there was one thing that sort of snapped me out of it," she said.

Having always read inspirational and motivational books, Debbie decided one day to go to a seminar about health, recovery, and attitude. A medical doctor was holding the seminar at a public school lunchroom on the city's west side. Debbie was one of about 150 people in attendance.

"The speaker started by going around the room asking each one of us to say why we were there in 20 words or less. After every one of us had spoken, he had listened to about 150 stories of mostly people who had cancer. After the last person spoke, he broke a brief silence by asking the question, 'Anybody want to switch?' That just blew me away, because not one person did, and of course I knew that my life was not a perfect life, but it was *my* life. I saw clearly that I had choices of what kind of day I could have. That very moment, I knew I would keep this one and I wanted it to become a building block. Although it took a little time, I think I got to the right place. I knew that with my breast cancer, the biggest thing that would help me was to try to do a little good for somebody else."

Describing that day and its effects, Debbie laughed out loud. "Then it started taking over my life!" she said. " I thought to myself, I will volunteer for one hour, then I will agree to be on a board committee, then I will volunteer for one day a week, and then I will see how far these pink ribbon pins will go."

Many people have seen the tiny pink enamel pins worn on a collar or lapel that serve as a reminder of the battle against breast cancer and the women who are fighting it. They are one of the best-selling items that my company offers to gift stores and department stores. Yesterday, we ordered 5,000 of them just to fill our orders. All these years, I wondered how they got started. Now I know.

Debbie Schatz, founder of the pink ribbon pin and the New York City company that sells and promotes it, came into her own during her encounter with breast cancer. Her story of life *after* breast cancer, not *because* of breast cancer, is the story of a woman who decided how she was going to use her life after cancer had changed it—she would make the most of each day. Her pins and other products, along with her volunteer work, serve as comfort, encouragement, and reminders to women who are facing breast cancer and to the people who love them. Debbie's life makes a difference in the lives of other people.

∽

Life is all about making choices. When confronted with breast cancer, you can decide to give up on life, or you can move into a new era—life after breast cancer. Make the most of each day. Decide how you are going to live your life from this moment on.

∽

*D*oves circle in the
clear blue sky, trying to find their way home.
The death of a loved one is not only a time for
grieving, it can also be a time for renewal of purpose.
God has a purpose for each of our lives. The death
of a loved one reminds us that God also has
a purpose for our death.

CHAPTER TWELVE

And They Flew

Run your race to win.
1 CORINTHIANS 9:24 (TLB)

STANDING AT THE KITCHEN SINK, I WASHED the last few dishes from our family's evening dinner. The table had been cleared. I was about to help our oldest son with some spelling words. Thinking ahead, I hoped that maybe I could squeeze in a bit of reading before it was time for going to bed. With my hands dripping wet from the dishwater, I felt frustrated that no one else in the house would answer the phone as it rang. I almost let it go on ringing, unanswered, but something told me this would be an important call. Reaching up, I grabbed a paper towel, and then the phone. As I placed the phone to my ear, I heard my sister's voice say, "I have some news I need to share with you."

My knees went weak as I slid into the nearby wooden chair to listen. This was one of those phone calls you never want to get.

My sister, a registered nurse, had always been dedicated to taking Mother and Daddy to their doctor's appointments. Today she had taken our mother. She always sat in on those appointments listening to what the doctors had to say, because sometimes her ears heard words that had to be explained to

Mother in common terms later. But today was different. The doctor's words were a simple, shocking statement. Mother had received a diagnosis of breast cancer too advanced for much treatment. The doctor would try to keep things as comfortable as possible, but he told us to count weeks instead of months.

My mother had been one of the strongest women I had ever known. She never complained, and when you asked her how she felt, her answer was, "Oh, all right." She had fallen and broken her hip several years ago and walked with a crutch ever since, but it never seemed to slow her spirit down.

Due to my mother's wishes, my sister and I never used the C-word in speaking of her illness. Born in an earlier generation, Mother was embarrassed that she had cancer, much less breast cancer. To all her close friends and church members, she only said she had congestive heart failure, and she never complained. My sister and I would just look at each other and bite our tongues, because we respected her wishes and realized that everyone handles the situation in their own way.

Mother's disease progressed quite rapidly, just as the doctor said it would, and the last few days Mother spent with us, the hospital gave her megadoses of medicine to help ease any pain. The long days and hours were hard on my father, who never left her side. Our son Samuel brought his Little League softball trophy to her bedside to show her. Although she never opened her eyes, she squeezed his hand. As the hours came to an end, I realized the best thing I could do was what I was doing, simply being there in her silent room with my father and sister as we mourned together.

That was two years ago, and I miss my mother terribly. I miss her helping my sons with math homework, because she had such patience that I never had. She would read for hours with a little boy in her lap. I miss her being just a phone call away when I am in the kitchen, because she was the most wonderful cook. I miss her listening ear when I called her with good news or bad. I wish that she had never had to suffer as she did in those last days. But because of mother's illness and all the time we spent together, we realized just how wonderful she was and how gracefully she bowed out.

> *The most important medicine*
> *is tender love and care.*
> MOTHER TERESA

Shouting from the Rooftops

That was then, and this is now. Now my sister and I shout from the rooftops about the advantages of simply getting a mammogram. At the same time Mother was in the hospital, I learned that one of our employees just down the hall—Val, a precious young mother—had been diagnosed with breast cancer too, through her yearly mammogram. And although Val's cancer was aggressive, it had been caught. Caught early enough to make a difference. Yes, Val would lose her hair, but her mother, husband, and children would not lose her.

Sometimes I honestly believe that as Mother slipped away, she knew God had a purpose not only for her life, but also for her death. With family and friends gathered all around us at her funeral, my sister, father, and I released white doves to circle the summer sky. As we walked away and looked up above the cemetery, I was surprised at how the doves seemed to linger as they circled and circled, trying to find their direction back home. The doves symbolized to me the Holy Spirit, and I knew my mother was in heaven.

Those July hours sitting in Mother's tiny hospital room listening only to the beep of a monitor gave me lots of time to think. Daylight and dark—the answer to stopping this disease was simple! Early detection with a mammogram and self-exam. The key to saving a life is education—for all wives, mothers, sisters, and friends—yet what could I do to make a difference?

With my husband's support, the manufacturing and import business that we own has become very active and supportive of breast cancer awareness. When I heard that taking such a simple test could be a life-saving decision, it was a rude awakening for me.

The following October I felt the urge to participate in the Susan G. Komen Race for the Cure. Early Saturday morning I made the drive to Little Rock's downtown festivities. I hunted and hunted to find a parking place, because I'd had no idea how many people were going to participate in the run. I had to walk several blocks to get to the starting point of the race, and as I approached I was not prepared for the two tables that lined the sidewalk. At one table you could pick up a sign to wear on your back during the race that read, *In honor of*_____. You were to fill in the blank with a felt-tip marker. I was overtaken with emotion at that table, because I did not want to go to the other table, where you could pick up a sign that read, *In memory of*_____. My heart was aching; I wanted to wear the sign that read, *In honor of* _____ and write in my mother's name, but of course I couldn't do that.

And so it is with a passion that I speak to groups of ladies as I travel around the country. I am not afraid to ask, "Have you had a yearly mammogram?" I am not ashamed to use the C-word, because I know we can make a difference with a simple test. I am able to say the words, *breast cancer*.

Last year, the company my husband and I own was a corporate sponsor of Little Rock's Race for the Cure. A huge 20-foot banner with the name of our company was draped over Main Street for the runners to pass under. The mayor of our capital city stood in a crane bucket, courtesy of the local electric company, that lifted him way up over the crowd. In his hand he held a microphone and prepared to shoot the starting gun for the thousands of runners spread out below. But the biggest surprise was yet to be.

Through the roar of the crowd among the sea of pink T-shirts, the moment came almost in slow motion, just like in the movies. The starter gun rang into the air. What I thought was a microphone turned out to be a cord, set to release a flock of white doves into the clear blue sky right over the banner with my company name on it. I had seen the doves circle and circle once before during that July day at the cemetery, and in that moment at the Race as I awaited their release, I knew God had a plan for me…and I knew my mother was watching.

The key to saving a life is education. Talk to friends, family, neighbors, and co-workers about breast cancer, get your mammogram, and remind other women that taking this simple test can be a life-saving decision.

"Come to the edge," he said.
They said, "We are afraid."
"Come to the edge," he said.
They came.
He pushed them...
And they flew.

GUILLAUME APOLLONAIRE

The Painter's Canvas
of a Day

I am given a blank canvas to paint my day in whatever colors I choose. The responsibilities that lie before me and the circumstances may not change, but I have control over the colors that I choose to paint my day.

I can paint my sky gray and gloomy,
or I can paint clouds of gray to water the earth.

I can paint sadness for my health
or I can gladden my heart, for I am alive.

I can paint the thorns on a rose bush,
or I can paint beautiful roses.

I can paint the mountains of work that lie before me,
Or I can be thankful that I have work to do.

I can choose red and paint anger with a friend,
or I can color my heart red with forgiveness,
And be thankful for my friends.

I can paint green with envy,
Or paint gold, the courage
God has blessed me with.

I am blessed with a palette of hope,
courage, kindness and peace.

It is all up to me, in the colors I choose
to paint my day.

ALDA ELLIS

Resources

Race for the Cure
www.raceforthecure.com

Susan G. Komen Breast Cancer Foundation
www.breastcancerinfo.com

Faces of Hope
www.facesofhope.com

National Breast Cancer Foundation
www.nationalbreastcancer.org

American Cancer Society
www.cancer.org

Avon's Breast Cancer Awareness Campaign
www.avoncrusade.com

National Alliance of Breast Cancer Organizations
www.nabco.org

Sisterhood Cards
Vicki Kovaleski Fine Art
P.O. Box 17275
Little Rock, AR 72212
www.kovaleskistudio.com

Debbie Schatz
www.pinkribbonjewelry.com